THE NIIHAU INCIDENT

Japanese Naval Airman 1st Class Shigenori Nishikaichi, crack fighter pilot from the carrier Hiryū. *After attacking Oahu, December 7, 1941, he was to meet with a bizarre misadventure on Niihau.*

The Niihau Incident

The true story of the Japanese fighter pilot who, after the Pearl Harbor attack, crash-landed on the Hawaiian Island of Niihau and terrorized the residents.

By Allan Beekman

Heritage Press of Pacific
1279-203 Ala Kapuna Street / Honolulu, Hawaii 96819

Second Printing, June 1983
Third Printing, April 1986
Fourth Printing, October 1987
Fifth Printing, May 1990

Library of Congress Catalog Card No. 82-83137

ISBN: 0-9609132-0-3

Published and distributed by:

Heritage Press of Pacific
1279-203 Ala Kapuna Street
Honolulu, Hawaii 96819

Also by Allan Beekman
HAWAIIAN TALES

Printed in the U.S.A. by Harlo Press, 50 Victor, Detroit, MI 48203

PRINCIPAL CHARACTERS

(The name underlined is that by which the character
is chiefly identified in the text).

Naval Airman 1st Class Shigenori Nishikaichi, Japanese
fighter pilot

Howard Kaleohano, Niihau cowboy

Aylmer Robinson, lord of Niihau

Ben Kanahele, Niihau cowboy

Ishimatsu Shintani, Niihau ranch hand

Yoshio Harada, Niihau beekeeper

Irene Umeno Harada, wife of Yoshio

1st Lt. Jack Mizuha, executive officer John Burns Field,
Kauai

Pfc. Ben Kobayashi, member of 299th Infantry

The pronunciation of the above names, and some others, is
given at the first mention of the name in the text. See Index.

CONTENTS

LIST OF ILLUSTRATIONS

Whosoever relieves or attempts to relieve the enemy with arms, ammunition, supplies, money or other things or knowingly harbors or protects or holds correspondence with or gives intelligence to the enemy, either directly or indirectly, shall suffer death or such other punishment as a courtmartial or military commission may direct.

81st Article of War

THE NIIHAU INCIDENT

1

THE ATTACK ON OAHU

Aboard the carrier *Hiryū*, 230 miles north and slightly east of the Island of Oahu, Hawaii, Naval Airman 1st Class Shigenori Nishikaichi (*pron.* shē-gā-nŏ'-rē . nē-shē-kî'-chē) watched the elevators hoist to the flight deck the planes scheduled for the second strike against Oahu. As it had when he had watched the first wave of planes take off in the predawn darkness of that fateful day of December 7, 1941, the carrier, beneath his feet, pitched and rolled in the mountainous seas.

At 6 a.m., Lt. Cmdr. Mitsuo Fuchida (*pron.* mē-tsū'-ō . fōō-chē'dä) had roared off the flight deck of the *Akagi* in a Mitsubishi 97 bomber to lead the first wave. Although a Zero had plunged into the sea from the heaving deck of the *Hiryū*, and a bomber from another carrier had developed engine trouble, the planes that followed had made a record launching.

Within 15 minutes, 43 fighters, 49 high-level bombers, 51 dive bombers and 40 torpedo bombers had been launched from the six carriers. With do-or-die resolution, without parachutes, the flyers had circled the fleet, swung into formation and headed for Oahu as the assembled crew members waved their hats and cheered.

From southern Japan, Fuchida had spent 25 of his 39 years in the Imperial Japanese Navy. He had first visited Hawaii in 1924, after graduating from the naval academy, Etajima. Veteran of air combat in China, he had logged more than 3,000 hours in the air.

The imminent attack on Oahu was the culmination of events strung over years that had at last brought Japanese-American relations to the breaking point. As a navy man, he tended to give more attention to military crises. From a military standpoint, perhaps the first step towards the final confrontation with America had occurred in September 1931 when Japan had begun occupying Manchuria. From a diplomatic standpoint, relations between Japan and America had taken a sharp turn for the worse when Japan had signed the Tripartite Pact with Germany and Italy, September 27, 1940.

In retaliation for Japan's Axis leanings and for its activities in China and Southeast Asia, President Franklin D. Roosevelt had imposed economic restrictions on Japan. Then, July 23, 1941, he had frozen all Japanese assets. August 1 he had embargoed the export of oil and gasoline to Japan, the British and Dutch following suit.

Since Japan must have oil or perish, she would attack the Dutch East Indies and British Malaya to take the needed raw materials she was unable to buy. The Japanese command believed that America had agreed to aid the British and Dutch if Japan attacked them. Consequently, to have a free hand for military operations against the British and Dutch, Japan believed she needed to destroy the American Pacific Fleet.

Admiral Isoroku Yamamoto, commander in chief of the Japanese Imperial Navy, planned to destroy the American Pacific Fleet at its base at Pearl Harbor, Oahu, Hawaii through a surprise aerial attack. In the pursuit of this objective, the Pearl Harbor Striking Force, under command of Vice Admiral Chūichi Nagumo, gathered, November 16, at the mouth of the Inland Sea.

Soon after dark, the armada began stealing out of Saiki Bay to rendezvous in the Kuril Islands, far to the north. To perform their assigned roles in the operation, 27 of Japan's "I" class submarines, between the 18th and 19th of November, set off in groups of three from their bases at Kure and Yokosuka.

Called "I" because a character from the alphabet resembling a small "i" preceded its identifying number, each submarine carried a seaplane for extra reconnaissance. In a large tube on each deck, five carried a midget submarine.

14

The midgets were supposed to steal into Pearl Harbor before the planned attack and launch their torpedoes after the attack began. The "I" submarines were to lurk outside of Pearl Harbor and torpedo any ship escaping after the attack began. They were also to sink supporting shipping from the mainland.

In addition, one "I" submarine was assigned to a rescue mission at Niihau (nē'-hou) Island, to the west of Kauai (kou'-ī) the most northern of the Hawaiian Islands.

If a plane became disabled over the combat area, the pilot was to pick the best target and crash on it. If a plane were able to make it to Niihau, believed by the Japanese to be uninhabited, the pilot was to crash-land there and await rescue by the "I" submarine. The submarine's seaplane would be able to land in the deep waters off Niihau.

Though Nishikaichi knew of this provision, some of the attacking flyers did not.

Thoughts of making a creditable showing during the coming attack were more on the mind of Nishikaichi, however, than plans for suicide or forced landing on Niihau. Since boyhood he had schooled himself for the role he was about to play.

He had been born April 21, 1920 in Hashihama, Imabari, Ehime Prefecture, Japan, the second son of Ryōtaro and Fusako Nishikaichi. The region faces the Inland Sea.

Though he had swum in these waters, his thoughts had early turned skyward. From the time he had taken his examination for entrance to Imabari Middle School, in March 1933, he had expressed his intention of becoming a naval flyer.

He studied diligently, but found time to become a member of the school boat crew and to gain second rank in jūdō. In the mornings, on his second-floor verandah, he practiced swinging a sword.

Militarism was on the march in Japan. Many ambitious youths were seeking military careers. But of 69 in Ehime who took the examination for Naval Aviation School only seven, he included, were chosen.

15

He entered the Yokotsuka Naval Training School where he enjoyed the austere life and rigorous training.

July 7, 1937 the smoldering dispute with China flared again. Soon it developed into undeclared war.

During this period, Nishikaichi was sent on a long cruise. He landed in Shanghai, which still smoldered from the conflict that had raged there. He saw skeletons of destroyed homes, honest citizens trembling in fear.

He wrote home, "Dear Father, never lose in war. The misery of the people of a defeated nation is truly pitiful."

At Kasumigaura flying school he began to fly for the first time, though only as a passenger. Finally his superiors assigned him to a fighter plane. As relations with America deteriorated, training intensified; the Navy transferred him to the Naval Aviation School in Ōita, afterwards to Ōmura Air Field.

In September 1941, he visited his parents for the last time. He was tall and hardened from years of training. It was common knowledge that Japanese-American relations were nearing the breaking point, but he evaded questions about the imminence of war. Nevertheless, his parents noticed his attitude differed from what it had been on previous visits.

He told his father, "It takes one million yen to make an aviator."

"My, what a sum! ... With all that money invested in you, for you to die without accomplishing anything would be worse than being disloyal."

His later actions would indicate this observation had struck a responsive chord. At the time he simply said, "If I'm to die, I want to pick a place in which it's worthwhile to die."

Returning to Ōita, he gained promotion to Naval Airman 1st Class. November 13, he wrote home that he was to be transferred; it would be a while before he could write again.

November 26 the fleet sailed from Tankan Bay in the Kuril Islands for the attack on Hawaii. The task force was the largest ever assembled up to that time. It included six carriers, two battleships, two heavy cruisers, a light cruiser and nine destroyers.

Even before leaving Tankan Bay, Nishikaichi had realized he was going on an important mission. About the same time he had developed serious leg pains. December 2 the command mustered the men and told them they were to attack the American fleet at Pearl Harbor. Nishikaichi feared his superiors might diagnose his leg pains as symptomatic of loss of nerve. The excruciating pains continuing, he wrote in his diary:

"Ah, that my leg pains may be healed by December 7! Only this worries me."

Again he wrote, "I must get well." Upon this resolution the pain disappeared.

He wrote to his parents: "What was my purpose in going through hard work to train my skill? It was for this day. People may have had doubt about me; God alone knew my ambition. I have no regrets."

He gave the letter to his friend and said, "If I die, take care of this. I'll take care of your letter. We have already given up our lives. But this is just in case either of us should return alive."

Before them lay the seven main islands of the Hawaiian archipelago like a strung bow bent in their direction, the bowstring pointing northeast. The lower limb of the bow lay to their right; below the center, where the grip would have been, was their target: Oahu. Farther to their right were the islands of Kauai and Niihau.

The attention of the attackers was directed almost solely towards Oahu, third largest of the islands. By virtue of its harbor Oahu was the most populous island. After the harbor had been discovered in 1784, in the then village of Honolulu, commerce had gravitated to it. By 1941, Honolulu had become a thriving, modern city with a population of 180,000 and was the capital of the Islands.

Seven miles west of Honolulu was Pearl Harbor, which had gained importance when sailing vessels began to give way to steamers fueled by coal. In 1941 Pearl Harbor could shelter and service America's largest battleships. As Japanese intelligence confirmed, this morning the American fleet was assembled there except for its carriers—*Saratoga, Lexington* and *Enterprise.*

17

The attackers knew that a successful attack on the fleet would involve more than going straight to the ships and bombing them. Oahu was a fortress bristling with airfields that might be expected to launch swarms of planes to defend the fleet. Consequently, of the 353 Japanese planes that would be launched, only 154 were assigned to attack American warships. The remaining 199 were charged with securing air superiority by bombing and strafing the American airfields and destroying, in the air or on the ground, any American aircraft.

Among the revelations with which the attackers would discomfort the defenders would be the performance of the Zero, A6M, single-seat fighter plane, one of which would be flown by Nishikaichi. Designed by Jirō Horikoshi for the Mitsubishi combine, this low-wing monoplane fighter was able to outclimb any other plane in Asia or the Pacific and to fight at greater heights.

The Zero carried cannon as well as two machine guns. It had twice the combat range of the standard American fighter, the P-40. In the hands of the superbly trained pilot who manned it, the Zero was superior to any fighter that could be pitted against it.

The *Hiryū* was to contribute 27 planes to the second attack, nine of them Zeros, 18 of them dive bombers.

All told, in the second wave there would be 171 planes—36 fighters, 54 high-level bombers and 81 dive bombers—under command of Lt. Cmdr. Shigekazu Shimazaki.

On the *Hiryū*, while the maintenance crews bustled about readying the planes, Lt. Sumio Nōno, in command of the squadron of fighters, had his pilots write down the direction and speed of the wind and data from the day's observation of the weather.

"Go!" came the command, "Do your best."

"Thanks, I'll do my best."

In the hands of the maintenance crew, Nishikaichi's plane, B11-120, awaited him, motor roaring.

With the other pilots, Nishikaichi whirled and raced for his plane.

Each fighter pilot climbed into his cockpit, exchanging places with his crew chief. As the planes began to take off, the crew lined the side of the carrier, waving caps, their cheers drowned by the roar of the motors.

Nishikaichi was to fly wing of the second section of Nōno's squadron. He fell into formation. The 18 dive bombers followed. The planes from all carriers assumed formation and headed for Oahu, the Zeros behind the *Hiryū* dive bombers, Nishikaichi to the right of the formation.

It was 7:30 a.m. The first wave had not yet reached Oahu.

Though the success of the operation was predicated on surprise, Fuchida believed surprise was unlikely to be achieved. Instead he expected to lose half his planes in the attack.

Fortune favored him. As he arrived over Kahuku Point, the northwest tip of Oahu, he found the weather flawless. Visibility was good. Clouds were mostly over the mountains, with a base of 3500 feet. The climatic conditions were ideal for the success of his mission.

Further, despite many clues and portents of the impending attack, the defenders were unalert to the danger. The Hawaiian commanders expected a surprise attack in the Japanese tradition. They even expected the blow to fall that weekend. But they expected the blow to fall in Southeast Asia.

Lt. Gen. Walter Campbell Short, commanding the Hawaiian Department, believed the most imminent danger to Hawaii was not aerial attack but sabotage.

This conviction derived, at least in part, from the manner in which the local authorities had developed and peopled Hawaii.

When Capt. James Cook had discovered the archipelago in 1778, he had named it the Sandwich Islands in honor of his patron, the Earl of Sandwich. Cook's crew had introduced venereal disease and other foreign ailments.

Lacking resistance to foreign disease, adapting imperfectly to the competitive culture of immigrating

Americans and Europeans, the native population had been seized by malaise. It rapidly declined in numbers.

Western newcomers found the islands suitable for the cultivation of sugar. To cultivate sugar, they introduced different nationalities on three-year contracts, keeping them docile by playing off these different national groups against each other.

Thus they brought in Japanese to keep down the earlier imported Chinese. December 7, 1941 there were about 160,000 persons of Japanese ancestry in Hawaii. Though only 24 percent of these were foreign born, the U.S. Census, press, radio and other sources listed the entire group as Japanese—37 percent of the total population.

Expecting a Japanese strike in Southeast Asia and concommitant attempts at sabotage in Hawaii by at least some elements of this large, supposedly foreign segment, Short had put his planes out in the open, wing tip to wing tip. There they could be effectively guarded against saboteurs. They would be open targets for aerial attackers.

Still ignorant of how the enemy had played into his hands, Fuchida listened to the light music from the Honolulu radio station he was using as a direction finder. Seeing no American planes, he concluded his pessimism had been unfounded; surprise was possible. At 7:49 he signalled for a surprise attack.

At 7:55 the Japanese dropped bombs on Hickam Field. At 7:57 the torpedo planes attacked battleships in Pearl Harbor. By 8:00, having met no enemy planes, the Zeros began strafing the air bases. At 8:05 the level bombers had at the reeling warships.

Still far north, the second wave knew that Fuchida, having achieved surprise, must be wreaking terrible destruction. When the Shimazaki group arrived at Kahuku Point at 8:40 they found the destruction continuing and received orders to orbit to avoid collisions with the first wave.

Within about an hour of the dropping of the first bombs the first wave finished its mission. At 8:45 Shimazaki gave the second wave the order to attack: "To! To! To!"

The formation curved to the right.

Lt. Cmdr. Takashige Egusa led 81 dive bombers over the Koolau Range to attack the warships in Pearl Harbor. Under command of Shimazaki, 54 level bombers split up to attack Hickam Field, the Kaneohe Naval Air Station and nearby Bellows Field. Nine bombers from the *Shokaku* were to undertake the Kaneohe-Bellows mission while protected and assisted by the Nishikaichi group of fighters. This fighter group had been reduced to eight because one had developed engine trouble and turned back.

The U.S. Naval Air Station at Kaneohe Bay encompassed an area that sticks out from southeastern Oahu like the head of a horse seen in profile. Ponds separate the head from the neck, with Mōkapu Point the tip of the ears at the eastern extremity and Pyramid Rock above the muzzle at the western. Behind the chin and below the cheek, facing the hangars, were the ramps the seaplanes traversed from the bay to dry land.

Like others in authority, Cmdr. Harold Montgomery Martin, commanding, had been concerned about the possibility of sabotage. On Friday, the 5th, he had been indirectly warned that the possibility was imminent. On the morning of the 6th, he had had the crew again addressed concerning this danger.

Under his command were 303 naval personnel plus 31 officers and 93 marines plus two marine officers.

The station included both the sea plane area and an air field. Assigned to the station were 36 PBY (Consolidated Catalina) type aircraft—the Navy patrol flying boat. As the Japanese drew near, three of these planes were out on patrol. Four were moored in Kaneohe Bay about a thousand yards apart. Four were in the No. 1 hangar. In one hangar was the regular watch of one ready-duty plane and a crew of about 30. The other planes were parked on the ramp.

Most of the crew were in their barracks or in Bachelor Officer Quarters.

When Fuchida had given the order to attack, Martin had been in his quarters in the seaward part of the station. From there he saw 12 Zeros approaching from slightly west of north, flying at about 800 feet.

The approaching group at first resembled an American carrier group preparing to land on the field. But contrary to station regulations, the planes made a right hand turn. As they did so, Martin's young son pointed out the red circles painted on the exposed fusilage.

Martin rushed for the administration building. But he had hardly left the house before the Japanese opened fire. The planes had come down to roof-top height, strafing the American planes with incendiary bullets. One attacking plane rose to shoot at the control tower on the high hill facing the sea. Within eight minutes, the Japanese riddled several small boats used for servicing and set all exposed American planes on fire.

Only a single machine gun returned the Japanese fire.

A telephone call to the 14th Naval District duty officer brought word that Pearl Harbor was being attacked.

Now at Kaneohe, fire apparatus and fire-fighting crews rushed to the burning planes. Assisted by a contractor's civilian personnel, they tried to drag the burning planes clear of the hangars. As rifles and machine guns were distributed, those receiving them rigged firearms on planes or temporary mounts.

Then directly seaward, from slightly east of north, came the second wave—the Nishikaichi group of eight Zeros escorting nine level bombers.

Preceding the bombers, the Zeros strafed the area, continuing strafing as the bombers glided in to drop their bombs, some incendiary. The bombs reignited the hangars, blowing up the planes lined up around them and killing a civilian heavy equipment operator as well as military personnel.

The Zeros then dropped lower, strafing the hangars and any planes undestroyed by the bombers. Fire from machine guns and rifles blasted at Nōno as he attacked a plane, but he strafed the plane and set it afire. Nishikaichi's section of three planes strafed a plane and destroyed a truck.

Nōno now reformed his squadron and, according to schedule, headed for Bellows Field, ten air miles down the coast.

Built on a coral reef formed when the ocean level was higher than it is now, Bellows was a small Army fighter base under command of Lt. Col. Leonard D. Weddington. Without a hanger, it had about eight observation planes and 12 modern P-40 fighters. Except for machine gun bullets, the post had no ammunition readily available.

Like the other stations, Bellows had been alerted for sabotage. Like the others, it had responded by neatly lining up the planes where they would be open targets from the air. There was no ground anti-aircraft defense.

About 8:35 a.m., in his home about a mile from the post, Weddington received word that the post had been attacked. A single Zero had strafed the field and wounded a medical detachment private in his bed in the tent area. The Zero had then disappeared in the direction of Kaneohe.

Weddington rushed to the scene. None of his planes were in the air. The 298th Infantry, Hawaiian National Guard, put two .30 caliber anti-aircraft machine guns into position in a hole at the end of the runway. Weddington issued all the machine guns available, and ordered the men, if attacked, to fire when ammunition became available.

This was the situation when the Nōno squadron appeared and found ten P-40s lined up. Seven had still not received the ammunition requisite for combat; three were about to take off to intercept the anticipated attack.

The Japanese began strafing, wounding one man, setting afire a gasoline truck and shooting down one officer who was getting into his plane preparatory to taking off. The ground crew scattered.

Narrowly evading Japanese fire, a second readied plane took wing. The Japanese immediately shot it down. Having begun to move over the field, a third continued on its course; as it left the ground, Japanese bullets exploded and burned it. In addition, the Japanese wounded one man, damaged an observation plane and hit another.

In the meantime, from the sister ship of the *Hiryū*, the *Sōryū*, came the 3rd Covering Fighter Squadron of nine Zeros under command of Lt. Fusata Iida. Near the Kaneohe Air Force Base, with the aid of Nōno's squadron, the *Sōryū* squadron intercepted and quickly destroyed six enemy planes. The Japanese then strafed the field, machine-gunning all enemy aircraft in sight.

Nōno waggled his wings to order his Squadron to reassemble. Attacking to the last, Nishikaichi was slow to comply. When he finally broke off his attack and followed, he found himself behind the *Sōryū* squadron.

The leader of the *Sōryū* squadron, Iida, 27, had flown as fighter pilot since September of 1939. He had fought against Chinese fighters. A handsome man, kind to his subordinates, Iida often reminded them of the rule that if disabled they must crash on an enemy target.

That very morning he had told his squadron, ''The most important thing for a true *samurai* is his last act. For example, if I receive fatal damage to my fuel tank, I will aim my plane to cause the greatest damage. Then, without thought for survival, I will throw myself on that target.''

The *Sōryū* squadron seems to have been unaware of the provision for disabled planes to land on Niihau.

An opportunity was about to challenge if Iida would practice what he preached.

Iida circled over Kaneohe Air Field until sure that his fighters were assembled in formation, a white spray of gasoline shooting from his plane the while. Then he closed the canopy of his cockpit and dove straight for the hangars.

As he dove, all guns below concentrated on him. Motor wide open, smoke pouring from his plane he disappeared into the smoke of the hangars and re-emerged to crash into Hawai'iloa Hill.

The exploding plane blew the body of Iida to bits. Bouncing and breaking, the dislodged engine rolled over and over.

Another Japanese plane crashed in Kailua Bay.

The fires at the base were now completely out of control. The No. 1 hangar would burn to its steel structural work. Except for the three PBY's on patrol, all planes had been destroyed or rendered unusable—though nine would be restored. Including the civilian heavy equipment operator, there were 17 American dead and 67 wounded.

To discourage American aircraft from locating the task

force through following the flight of the returning planes, the Japanese pilots had been instructed to fly back circuitously. One group was to fly 20 miles south from Oahu before swinging in a wide circle to fly north. The *Sōryū* group was to fly 30 miles west before turning north.

After this detour, the planes were to rendezvous about 20 miles north of Kahuku Point.

Having low-powered radios, no navigator and no homing device, the Zeros were expected to have difficulty finding their way back to the carriers. Of course the Japanese fleet, to preserve the secrecy of its position was observing radio silence and would continue to do so. Consequently, the Zeros were expected to find a bomber at the rendezvous point to guide them back to the carriers.

On the death of Iida, Lt. j.g. Iyozo Fujita succeeded to command of the 3rd Covering Fighter Squadron. He began to lead it to the rendezvous point when nine American planes pounced on the Japanese formation from above.

Identifying the American planes as P36's, fighters, the Nōno squadron split right and left to counterattack. The *Sōryū* squadron joined in. The battle whirled left and right.

The slow, undergunned American planes were no match for the Zeros. As the Japanese planes shot them down, the American planes fell, trailing smoke. But the battle broke up the Japanese formation.

Nishikaichi had shot down an enemy plane. Six enemy bullets had punctured his plane, one bullet narrowly missing his knee. Though he may have been unaware of it, one bullet had punctured his gas tank about one-quarter of the way up so that gas was escaping. His engine would stall then start up again.

The second wave had been attacking for almost an hour. Now, at 9:45, it began to retire. Speed failing, Nishikaichi gradually fell behind the other planes.

When he reached the rendezvous point, he saw not a single Japanese plane. But as he flew on he noticed a Zero following, trailing white smoke.

The following Zero was that of Navy Airman 2nd Class Saburō Ishii, who had flown third wing of the Iida squadron.

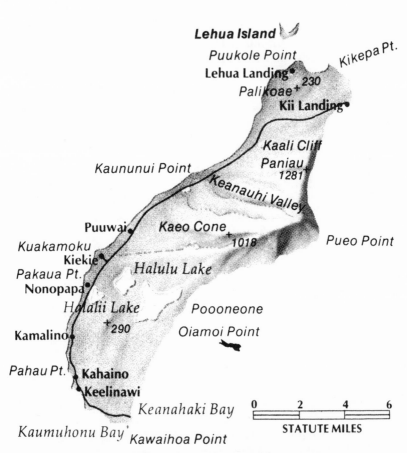

Lehua Island

Puukole Point
Lehua Landing•
Palikoae +230
Kikepa Pt.
Kii Landing•

Kaali Cliff
Paniau
1281+

Kaununui Point

Keanauhi Valley

Puuwai•
Kaeo Cone
+1018
Pueo Point

Kuakamoku
Kiekie•
Pakaua Pt.
Nonopapa•
Halulu Lake

Halalii Lake
+290
Poooneone
Oiamoi Point

Kamalino•

Pahau Pt.
Kahaino•
Keelinawi•
Keanahaki Bay

Kaumuhonu Bay
Kawaihoa Point

| 0 | 2 | 4 | 6 |
STATUTE MILES

*Map of Niihau, the mystery island of Hawaii
where the tragedy occurred.*

The likelihood of the crippled Ishii making it back to the carrier seemed remote, that of the Nishikaichi plane little better.

The aeronautic map Nishikaichi carried in the knee pocket of his flight suit showed about 124 miles of ocean separating Oahu from Niihau. Even at his reduced speed he could reach Niihau in 30 minutes.

On his right he caught sight of Kauai, called the Garden Island because of its lush natural greenery. Beyond, as he continued west, he discovered Niihau basking in the blue sea like a seal with upraised head, mountains and cliffs lava black, the rest of the island in various hues of green.

If the shape of Niihau is likened to that of a seal, the nose points toward Kauai. Travelling up the far side of Niihau, at what would be the base of the seal's spine, he saw, at Kiekie (Kē'-ā-kē'-ā) a fine ranch house with out buildings. Farther up the spine he found a cluster of modest frame houses, the village of Puuwai (pōō-ōō-wä'-ē). The natives were gathering before a frame church, the men in white shirts, white pants and white shoes. Even from the plane he could recognize that these stalwart men and stout women were of Polynesian type.

Nowhere did he see a plane.

Disheartened at finding wrong the official Japanese assumption that the island was uninhabited, he circled the island once and then flew out to sea toward the 22-mile distant small, bare, rocky islet of Kaula to the southwest. Still leaking gasoline, the other plane followed. His own engine coughed.

He recognized the futility of trying to reach the carrier, which now must be moving away from Hawaii.

Meaning to instruct the following plane to crash-land on Niihau, he signalled, "Go back."

Ishii waved a hand in negation. He had wired his carrier, ". . . Plane position lost."

Nishikaichi interpreted the gesture either to mean that the other wanted to follow or to land on Niihau together with him.

Confused, Nishikaichi continued north. He decided to

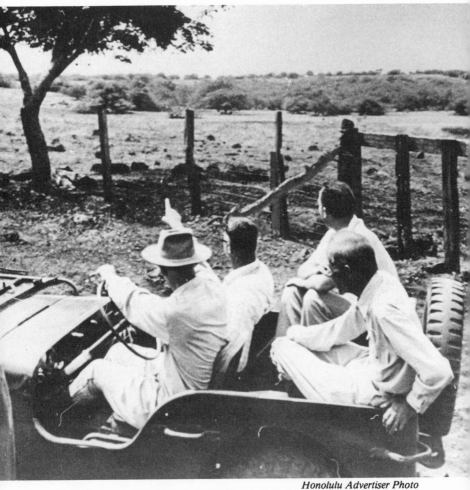

Honolulu Advertiser Photo

In this 1961 photograph, Lester Robinson points out to visiting Gov. William F. Quinn where Nishikaichi landed on Niihau.

avoid dying in vain; instead he would crash-land on Niihau with the other plane. He curved 180 degrees to the left.

Ishii wired the carrier, "My fuel is exhausted. I'll return to Oahu and self-destruct." He followed the lead of Nishikaichi, but then suddenly put his plane into a steep climb, circled once and plunged straight toward a reef, leaving a white spray.

When the spray subsided, the tail of the plane stuck out of the water to mark the grave of the pilot.

Still hoping to catch sight of the rescue submarine, Nishikaichi retraced the course he had flown. He turned inland, avoiding the ranch house. He hovered over the village and the adjoining pasture, frequently coming low as he searched for a suitable landing place.

Thousands of acres of pasture had been furrowed. And here and there rocks had been piled, making landing even more hazardous.

His gas exhausted, he picked what seemed the least dangerous landing place, an area a few hundred feet below the village that appeared, from the plane, to be a grassy slope.

If he survived the landing, he might be able to make friends with the natives. The place would be suitable from which to maintain a lookout for the submarine and its scout plane.

He pulled on his control stick. A wire fence snagged the landing wheels and tore them off. The plane pitched forward on its nose, the impact breaking loose the pilot's harness and knocking him unconscious.

2

HOWARD KALEOHANO AND NIIHAU

As the plane of Nishikaichi had descended to land, Howard Kaleohano had been standing in his front yard watching the skittish antics of his horse, which was tethered nearby. The animal had taken fright at the sound of the approaching plane. As the plane wheels struck the fence, there came a sudden whoosh and boom. The terrified horse broke its tether and fled.

Howard whirled round and saw the plane, 20 feet away, pitched forward on its nose. He ran to it, pulled out the dazed pilot and relieved him of pistol and papers.

Though Howard knew nothing of the Oahu attack, he was one of the most intelligent and best-informed residents of the island.

Born in Kona, Island of Hawaii, October 16, 1912, Howard had been educated in the Alae Elementary School to the 8th grade. Unlike most other residents, he spoke English as his mother tongue.

In 1930, he had come to Niihau to visit a sister, Mrs. Moses Keale (Kelly). Like everyone else choosing to visit Niihau, he had had to apply to the manager, Aylmer (īl'-mer) Robinson, member of the family that owned the island.

Aylmer, 53, resided at Makaweli, Kauai. Niihau, which he visited once a week, was his domain; its residents his wards. He ran it as his ancestors had done, discouraging intrusions and keeping the life of his wards Spartan and primitive.

30

Howard Kaleohano, one of the most intelligent and best-informed of the residents of Niihau.

After passing the physical examination required of anyone granted permission to visit the island, Howard received passage aboard the sampan Aylmer used for his visits. The sampan took food and mail for the 136 residents. It made the trip from Makaweli to Nonopapa Landing, on the western side of Niihau, below Kiekie, in four and a half hours.

Nonopapa is the best landing on Niihau, but it is usable only in summer. In winter Aylmer used the Kii (kē'-ē) landing on the side of Niihau facing Kauai.

Westernmost of the eight Hawaiian islands, Niihau lies about 17.5 miles across the Kaulakahi Channel from Kauai. Eighteen miles long and up to six miles wide, it has a total of 73 square miles. The island is low at both ends. If we continue the analogy of its seal-like shape, the neck, shoulder and flipper is high tableland, rising to 1,281 feet at its highest point on the clifflike shore facing the channel. Here is Paniau, which will later figure in our story.

Since it is leeward of Kauai, on which the trades spend most of their moisture, subtropical, semi-desert Niihau receives only ten to 15 inches of rain a year. It is hot, dry, dusty and swarming with flies.

A map might show a string of lakes across the island, but they are lakes only during the rainy season, from December through March. At that time they fill up with brackish water suitable for drinking by animals. The rest of the year they appear as mud flats. Elsewhere there are similar, but smaller, mud flats, in which water holes appear in winter.

On the plain there are several minor springs. The largest perennial spring is Waiokanaio, about 500 feet up the northern wall of the Waiokanaio Gulch. From a collection tank at about 570 feet, the ranch pumps the water to about 1,100 feet to supply the stock.

During dry spells, Aylmer sometimes hauled water from Kauai in water tanks on sampans.

To compensate its 1500 shorthorn cattle and 12,000 merino sheep for the aridity of the island, the Robinsons had introduced Arizona cacti whose pulpy leaves provided food for the stock and supplemented the meager water supply.

Typical house, Puuwai, Niihau

The residents lived in the village of Puuwai in frame cottages, set far apart, each surrounded by a yard and enclosed within a lava-rock wall. For conserving water, caught during the rainy season, each house was equipped with a 1000-gallon storage tank.

The residents were chiefly of Polynesian stock, descendents of generations born and bred on the same island. The people being so few, intermarriage may have been inevitable. The Robinsons had tabooed the traditional Polynesian brother-sister marriages, but marriages of cousins, uncle with niece, aunt with nephew were permissible and practiced.

Some Niihauans had friends on other islands and even left Niihau to visit them. Some of the men worked on Inter-Island steamers, some such even rising to become officers. Some sailed on ships to mainland America and even to foreign countries. But in the main, most Niihauans never left the island. A midwife delivered them; their expectations never went beyond the nearby waters of their island.

Niihau-born Edward M. Kahale, a graduate of the Territorial Normal School in Honolulu, taught the children in the frame schoolhouse adjacent to the church. He was the only gainfully employed person on the island not on the Robinson payroll. The Robinsons owned the school building and the land it stood on.

Kahale taught his charges through the fourth grade. But of the 20 or so pupils, most dropped out in the third grade. The language of instruction was English, but except when engaged in school activity the children spoke in the aboriginal tongue.

After leaving school, the pupils quickly forgot English and much of what else they might have learned. Most of the population was illiterate.

A child of ten might begin to earn. There were about 45 cowboys on the payroll. All the men were expert horsemen. When a native son reached the age of 15 or 16, he naturally went to work as cowboy.

In the morning as the men reported for work, the foreman would assign tasks for them—one to drive turkeys, another to collect honey, another to clean out some of the water holes, another to check the sheep for blow flies. Despite constant treatment, blow flies, attacking sheep after wet weather, caused great loss.

In addition to the average run of horses, there were Arabian, originally brought from India and Australia.

The men wore Levis and cowboy hats. Each carried a six-inch hunting knife at his belt.

Captain Cook first set foot in the archipelago at Waimea, Kauai, January 19, 1778. A week later he crossed the channel and landed on Niihau.

He released goats on Niihau; they multiplied and soon ate most of the vegetation. Then heavy rains caused soil erosion, stripping large upland areas to hardpan and bedrock. Washed down into the lowlands, the red soil filled up the shallow ponds and bays.

The Robinsons slowed erosion by reforesting the uplands and assigning men to exterminate the goats. The goats exterminated, the Robinsons banned firearms.

The only firearms remaining were a double-barreled shotgun, with shells available, and a pistol without ammunition. Both guns were stored at the ranch house.

The Niihauans had once raised pigs. The Robinsons ordered the pigs turned loose to forage on the land. The pigs became feral.

When a man saw a pig, he would chase it down from horseback. When he had exhausted the pig, the hunter would dismount, turn the pig over and cut its throat.

Dogs were prohibited for fear they would become feral and prey on the sheep. Domesticated cats had become feral; they, as well as rats, preyed on the birdlife of the island, which was, nevertheless, abundant.

There were many peafowl. Thousands of turkeys roamed loose. There were ducks, plover, turnstone and curlew. Imported birds included prairie chicken, pheasant, California valley quail, mynah, partridge and Western meadow lark.

The island is luckily free of the mongoose that elsewhere in Hawaii preys on birds.

Beekeeping was an important occupation. Besides

35

several tons of wax, the island produced 1,200 cases (80 tons) of honey annually.

The men were paid once a month. Payday began at three in the afternoon and continued until nine or later. It was a kind of social gathering. All came and found occasion to eat while waiting.

Sundays were supposed to be exclusively for rest and church. On the Sabbath the natives were supposed to forego such gainful or pleasurable activities as riding, swimming, fishing, hunting or picking shells. Except for church, they were supposed to abstain from playing their ukuleles and guitars, at which they were expert.

They faithfully observed church attendance. The church was non-denominational but close to Congregational. The men came wearing white shirts, white pants, white shoes and astride horses. When they dismounted the seat of their pants would be stained with the red dust that had gathered on the saddle.

In church they listened to the reading from the Bible and sang hymns, beautifully, in their vowel-rich, melodious tongue. Bibles were numerous on the island, all in the aboriginal language—exact copies of the first missionary Bible published in Honolulu in the early part of the 19th century.

Morning and night every home held a prayer meeting. If the father had to leave home at 4 a.m., the family got up in time for the prayer meeting before he left.

The women were fat. They dressed nondescriptly, without regard to style, in something resembling a Mother Hubbard. They took care of the homes and earned money weaving makaloa mats, stringing necklaces of the pupu shells picked up from the beaches and making leis, from peacock feathers, for hatbands. They exported these products to Honolulu.

There was no police, no jail, no court, no movie, no alcohol. The sole electricity and radio was in the house of the ranch superintendent—paymaster John Rennie, adjacent to the ranch house. Born in Scotland, March 2, 1861, Rennie

36

Honolulu Advertiser Photo

The social life of Niihau centered around the church, right. Schoolhouse is at left. In this 1961 photograph residents await the arrival of Gov. William F. Quinn.

had been a supervisor for the Robinsons for more than 30 years at the time Howard arrived.

The Robinsons had given up residence in the ranch house years before when they had decided to remove from Niihau to Kauai. Now the ranch house was used only occasionally by Aylmer and his guests.

It was a rambling, old-style country home. The first portions had been brought around Cape Horn in 1864. Bit by bit the owners had added to the original residence until it came to have more than 19 rooms, not counting bathrooms, as well as many passageways and porches. Adjacent to it was not only the house of the ranch manager, Rennie, but other buildings such as servants' quarters, warehouses, carriage shed and honey house.

Occasionally vessels called to take away the products of beef, mutton and honey. Sometimes, too, when the situation seemed to justify such effort, the brawny arms of a native crew propelled a lifeboat across the channel to get supplies.

In these surroundings, where anyone who read the Bible in the aboriginal tongue was considered a scholar, the intelligence, learning and sophistication of Howard merited respect. He married Mabel Kahale, daughter of the schoolmaster, and became a cowboy. He had had some knowledge of the local language before arrival; he began to pick up the language and would, eventually, have equal mastery with that of the others.

He read the daily newspapers that Aylmer brought with him on his weekly visits. At the time Nishikaichi landed, Howard was aware of the strained relations between America and Japan. He had particularly taken notice of the passage through Honolulu of the Japanese diplomat Saburō Kurusu to assist Japanese Ambassador Kichisaburō Nomura in seeking to break the impasse between the two countries.

Now 29, about five feet six and a half inches in height, weighing about 140 pounds, Howard was strong and vigorous. Having disarmed his visitor, Howard became animated by concern for him. He led him, in friendly fashion, towards the house. Nishikaichi was the taller of the two but may have weighed five pounds less.

For five years, Nishikaichi had studied English as a literary language. Within limits he could read and write it; he spoke it with difficulty and understood little. It took him time to frame a question in the unfamiliar tongue.

As they neared the house, Nishikaichi asked, "Are you a Japanese?"

The question was a gambit in what was to become a search for a confederate.

The question was reasonable. Except for the darkness of his skin, Howard might have passed for a Japanese.

"No. I am a Hawaiian."

This answer might have mystified someone who spoke English as his mother tongue. Hawaii is a geographical area governed by America. Those born in it are American citizens by birth. It would be reasonable to assume that all persons born and bred in Hawaii are Hawaiian. But according to the concept with which the local authorities had indoctrinated Howard from the cradle upward, only the aborigines are Hawaiian.

Nevertheless, despite his mystifying statement, Howard's denial of being Japanese made clear to the pilot that he was not with a potential ally.

Before leaving the house, Mabel had made batter for pancakes. Now Howard offered the pilot black coffee, fried fish and pancakes with honey. Nishikaichi declined the honey but drank two cups of coffee and ravenously ate the fish and pancakes.

Nishikaichi drew out Japanese money and tried to pay for what he had eaten.

"No," said Howard, pointing to the strange money, "we can't use that here."

Had he been able to use the money, he might have still declined it. Generosity was a characteristic of the Niihauans.

Nishikaichi offered his host a Japanese cigarette. Howard declined. Instead, he drew out a bag of Bull Durham and rolled a cigarette. They smoked.

Evidently having pondered over a matter of deep concern and finding a means of expressing it, the pilot said, "Give paper back."

Howard declined.

Oral communication being too difficult, Nishikaichi struck on a better method. He drew out his notebook and wrote his request, handing the notebook to Howard for a written reply.

Howard wrote, "I cannot give the papers."

In the meantime, in search of an explanation for the landed plane, neighbors had begun to crowd around the house. Entering, they surrounded the pilot and tried to read what he had written. Most being illiterate, they tried in vain.

They bethought themselves of a better means of communicating with their visitor. The pilot was Japanese. There were three persons on the island who could speak this language. They would call one to act as interpreter.

The seemingly most appropriate interpreter would be Ishimatsu Shintani (ē-shē-mä′-tsū .shin-tä-nē). He had been born Nov. 17, 1881 in Takehara-chō, Kamo-gun, Hiroshima prefecture, Japan. As a younger son, he may have thought it prudent to seek his fortune abroad. He arrived in Hawaii January 24, 1900.

Sometime thereafter he came to Niihau, received permission to remain, married a local woman and began raising a family. He was happy to see his three children growing up around him. The communal life was similar to what had existed in the villages of Japan. Loyalty to the Robinson family, and to Aylmer Robinson as its head, was akin to the feudal system of those villages.

There existed what, generally, he must have regarded as no more than a slight flaw in his happiness. American law barred him from citizenship; further, it divested his wife of her citizenship because of her marriage to him. On the other hand, his children had become citizens at birth. He headed a house divided. Yet until today this situation must have seemed only a legal technicality without bearing on his daily life.

The messenger dispatched to summon Shintani would arouse in him the fears that he had buried in his heart and now might come forth to torment him.

Howard capitalized on the diversion to go out and inspect the plane.

In addition to the sheared landing gear, the propeller was bent. There were six holes in the fusilage. The pilot had not exhausted his ammunition; there were machine-gun shells and shells for the cannon. Against the background of strained Japanese-American relations, the appearance of this plane, seemingly riddled by bullets, appeared sinister.

By this time, Shintani had arrived. He had been briefed on the situation and approached his task with evidence of acute distaste. He and the pilot exchanged a few words. Shintani paled; the pilot froze. Shintani unhappily departed.

Puzzled, but believing they still might get the desired information from the pilot, the Niihauans thought of Yoshio Harada (yō-shē-ō hä-rä'-dä). Two young men mounted an unsaddled horse and galloped off to fetch him.

Ishimatsu Shintani. He headed a house divided. American law barred him from citizenship; it had divested his native wife of citizenship because of her marriage to him.

3

NISHIKAICHI AND THE HARADAS

Farmer Kikuyo Harada, with his wife Mii and infant daughter, Katsu, had arrived in Hawaii from his native Fukushima, Japan, November 7, 1899. The preceding year Hawaii had become a territory of the United States. Harada was one of a great number of Japanese laborers the planters hurriedly imported before the soon to be imposed American law would prohibit contract labor.

The transformation of Hawaii from native monarchy to American territory had been achieved in two stages. In the first stage, the white elite, becoming dissatisfied with the monarchy, had overthrown it in January 1893 and applied for annexation to America. Ashamed to admit an area in control of an illegal revolutionary government, America had denied the request.

The revolutionaries thereupon proclaimed the Republic of Hawaii, an oligarchy in which the qualifications for voting and holding office were so stringent that few natives and no Orientals could vote. Fewer still were eligible to serve in either house of the legislature.

In general, the planters had opposed annexation on the ground it would interfere with their system of importing and controlling labor. Now they came round to thinking that annexation with its assurance that their sugar could be imported to America duty-free was better than anarchy and more urgent than the need of keeping down the labor force.

After the election to the presidency in 1896 of William McKinley, the local authorities renewed negotiations for annexation. Congress granted annexation in 1898, Hawaii to become a Territory governed under the Organic Act, which would be enacted in April 1900.

The Organic Act abrogated the contracts by which the planters had held their laborers in bondage. It also prohibited further importation of contract labor.

From the first there had been a drain on the Japanese labor supply by laborers returning to Japan upon expiration of their contracts. Some chose to remain in Hawaii, but even among these most tended to leave the plantation.

With annexation, the laborers began leaving the plantations en masse. Many planned to go to the West Coast of America where pay and working conditions were supposed to be better. Seeing the laborers leaving, on whose sweating backs they had built their fortunes, the distressed planters sought relief by, on the one hand, trying to prevent the laborers from leaving and, on the other, encouraging mainland America to refuse them entry.

To invoke the first step, they passed a law discouraging recruitment of local labor by mainland agents; to ensure the second, they fanned the flames of Oriental prejudice on the West Coast. Despite such measures, many Japanese did emigrate from Hawaii to the mainland.

After the American flag was raised over Hawaii, any children born to the Japanese immigrants became American citizens at birth. The parents were barred by American law from becoming citizens; consequently, the children, at birth, also became subjects of Japan.

This condition of dual citizenship for the children of Japanese nationals was to continue until 1924. In that year, Japan abolished the system of automatically granting citizenship to children of her nationals abroad.

The system of dual citizenship played into the hands of the local authorities who, from the granting of annexation, made clear they would govern Hawaii in a spirit antithetical to the tradition of America. Hawaii was to be a no man's land. Only the aborigines would be recognized as Hawaiian.

Persons of Asiatic origin were to be carefully indoctrinated with the belief that for them race and nationality were one, the nationality to be the same as that of their foreign-born parents, the offspring being genetically disqualified from being anything else.

The local authorities inveigled Washington into furthering the conspiracy. Responding to the blandishments, the U.S. Census Bureau required all Nikkei (nēk-kā'-ē: person or persons of Japanese ancestry) to register as of Japanese nationality, fine and imprisonment the penalty for refusal.

The public schools registered the Nikkei, born under the American flag, as of Japanese nationality. The authorities exposed the Nikkei, from the cradle upward, to the doctrine that they were foreigners in the land of their birth. The Nikkei heard the doctrine in the schoolroom, they read it in the press, they gleaned it from the legislators, they saw it evidenced in the courts.

This was the environment into which Yoshio Harada was born at Waimea, Kauai, February 22, 1903. When his parents, Kikuyo and Mii, left Japan for Hawaii they had left behind three sons. The first of the family to be born on American soil, Yoshio was the fourth son and fifth child. Three more sons, and two daughters, would be born to the couple in Waimea.

On the plantation where Harada was born, the whites lived apart as an elite group. Class distinctions and respect for status were part of Japanese culture. But the difference in status between white plantation manager and Japanese laborer in Hawaii was greater than that between feudal lord and commoner in Japan. Before American law had abrogated the contracts that bound the Japanese to the plantations, the relation between manager and laborer was similar to that of a southern plantation owner and his slaves. On some plantations, mounted overseers carried bullwhips and used them to prod the laborers to greater industry.

Growing up in such a society, it was natural for Harada to try to seek out something better. It was strange, however, that he went to look for it in California, a State notorious for discriminatory laws against the Nikkei.

44

*Yoshio Harada. Big and husky for a
Nisei, handsome and well-liked, he
returned to Hawaii to marry Irene
Umeno Harada.*

On the West Coast of America, discrimination had formed around the Chinese who had preceded the Japanese. Especially since the disgruntled planters of Hawaii had lent themselves to the program, Japanese emigrating to California fell heir to the system.

The emergence of Japan as a military power after the Russo-Japanese War of 1904-5, brought on the Nikkei an even more virulent form of xenophobia, which crystallized into the Yellow Peril concept enunciated by Kaiser Wilhelm II of Germany. Irresponsible labor leaders and wild-eyed political demagogues fastened on the Nikkei as responsible for the evils of society and belabored them as whipping boys. California tried to put them in segregated schools. It passed legislation barring Japanese nationals from owning land. It prohibited Nikkei from marrying whites. It segregated them in public theaters. It restricted their use of public facilities such as swimming pools.

In 1924 the U.S. Congress gratuitously insulted the Japanese, and by implication their American-born offspring, by passing a Japanese Exclusion Law prohibiting further Japanese immigration.

Despite such harassment, which included discrimination in employment, Harada spent seven years in California, in Los Angeles and elsewhere.

He returned to Hawaii to marry Umeno Tanaka (ōō-mā'-nō .tä-nä-kä), daughter of Zensuke and Wasa Tanaka, who ran a jewelry store in Kapaa, Kauai. Farmer Zensuke, then 29, had arrived in Hawaii with his wife, Wasa, in September 1889 as a contract laborer for the sugar planters. He had left his son, Ichirō behind to be attended to by an uncle. While Hawaii was still the Kingdom of Hawaii, two daughters were born to the Tanakas. A son, Hajime, was born after the revolutionists had established the Republic. Umeno, who would later acquire the name Irene, was born February 17, 1905, the first of the family to be born on American soil.

The rural nature of Kauai may have contributed to the preponderance of Nikkei there. According to the Census statistics of 1940, there were 15,470 of them—43.2% of the total island population of 35,818. Among this proportionately great number, many of whom had been born and reared in Japan, there was frequent opportunity to speak Japanese and to observe the customs and traditions of Japan.

Among them it came to be understood that the Japanese language, disdained by their overlords, was a repository in which to secrete and keep hidden things that might embarrass the Nikkei if revealed to those outside the group.

To this foreignization, of course, was added the efforts of the local authorities. They applied to Irene the same indoctrination they had inflicted on Harada.

He had attended Japanese language school for an hour a day for eight years, insufficient to gain more than a rudimentary knowledge of the difficult written language. But he spoke Japanese fluently. She had attended Japanese language school through middle school.

He had never been in Japan. In 1928, at about age 22, she had travelled in Japan for nine months with her mother. Because of her mother's ignorance, Irene had acted as guide.

She had taken her mother to the home of Ichirō Tanaka, Irene's brother, in Yamaguchi prefecture. Ichirō was bitter because he had been palmed off on an uncle instead of being brought up as one of the original family.

It was the first time he had seen his family in all these years. He wanted Irene to remain. He dug up various marital prospects for her, some of whom she regarded as fairly good. But she wanted to return to Hawaii after her tour.

She and her mother travelled all over Japan. All the responsibility for travel arrangements fell on Irene. Sometimes she had difficulty reading the signs and figuring out the train schedules.

She visited Shikoku, the big island on which Nishikaichi had been born. She even visited his native prefecture, Ehime.

She was impressed by the great number of Buddhist pilgrims she saw in Shikoku. They dressed in simple, white kimono and wore white mittens and white leggings. They were followers of the great Buddhist priest Kūkai, posthumously named Kōbō Daishi who was born in

Sanuki province, now Kagawa prefecture of Shikoku, in A.D. 774.

Scattered about Shikoku are 88 Buddhist temples founded by Kōbō Daishi or closely related to him. Twenty-six of these temples are in Ehime Prefecture. The pilgrims visited each of these temples, travelling on foot and taking from 45 to 60 days to complete their pilgrimage.

Long after she returned to Hawaii the memory of these pilgrims remained with Irene.

When Harada returned to Kauai, he was five feet seven, big and husky for a Nisei (nē-sā: second generation. As used in this text it denotes a Nikkei born of immigrant parents). A sumō wrestler, handsome and well-liked, he put his strength to work as a stevedore at Port Allen.

Before his marriage to Irene, his parents had returned to their native Fukushima to live. She would never meet them. He and Irene established a home and brought forth three children.

In 1937, Charles Rice chose Harada over 19 other applicants to drive a Shell Oil truck. He had been on this job only three months when he was presented with what seemed a better offer.

A relative of Harada, said to have introduced beekeeping to Hawaii, had learned that Aylmer was looking for a beekeeper for Niihau. The relative recommended Harada. About July 1938, Aylmer called on the Haradas.

Aylmer offered the couple work on Niihau on a contractual basis. Irene was to keep house for Rennie. The couple could run a store and raise bees.

Harada saw in the offer an opportunity to save money and so to fulfill his ambition of returning, with wife and children, to the mainland. The contract was to run for 10 years. The term seemed excessive, but Aylmer might be persuaded to shorten it.

Irene was cool to the proposal. They were doing well on Kauai. The school on Niihau was substandard. There were no medical facilities there.

"What if my children get sick?" she protested.

"You don't need to worry," Aylmer told her, "If someone gets sick, the Hawaiians will signal Kauai with torches. Then a boat will come and take him to the hospital."

Nevertheless, she continued to think of life on Niihau as exile, as banishment from civilization and most of the associations she knew and loved. Aylmer continued his solicitation; Harada continued to persuade her. The length of the contract was shortened to five years. After seven months of resistance, Irene gave in.

The Haradas went to the hospital where they passed the rigid physical examination required of anyone being admitted to Niihau. They were to learn that when an outsider was permitted to ride the boat to Niihau, the Robinsons afterward disinfected the boat.

Harada's employer told him, "Anytime you want to come back, the job is here waiting for you."

Since all the Harada children were of kindergarten age or below, she took all three. Later Irene's older sister, Haruyo (Tanaka) Saiki, would ask to take care of one child; then feeling that child would be less lonely because of it, she asked for a second child. In the end, Irene would have with her only the youngest, a girl, Taeko (tä-ā'-kō).

In January 1939, the Haradas took up residence on Niihau. Rennie lived in a house originally occupied by the Robinsons. There were servants' quarters, but since Rennie was so glad to have their company, and he only wanting to reserve one room for himself, they had the run of this house.

Almost 78 when the Haradas moved in, Rennie was plagued with ill-fitting false teeth. To eat, he took out his teeth. Since the former cook had not adjusted the diet to this impaired ability to masticate, Rennie had been unable to eat some of the tougher morsels served him. He was malnourished and approaching feebleness.

Aylmer sent his own cook to teach Irene how to cook for the ranch. Mastering the craft, she fed Rennie on soft food he was able to eat easily. His health began to improve.

He took a great fancy to Taeko. He fell into the habit of taking her with him when he set out in his wagon, driven by a Niihauan, to make his rounds of the ranch.

By 1940 there were 1,615 hives of bees, 14,434 sheep, 955

cattle, 386 horses and mules. The human residents had increased in number; by 1940 there were 182.

Rennie had felt the gathering war clouds between Japan and America. Considering the possibility of a Japanese attack on Hawaii, both Army and Navy had recognized that in such case the Japanese might try to use Niihau as a landing place for their planes. To thwart such an attempt, the Army persuaded Aylmer to furrow the most appropriate terrain and place obstructions at appropriate points. The wreck of Nishikaichi's plane in landing attests to the effectiveness of the project.

To avoid alarming the Niihauans, Aylmer told them the furrowing was done to plant a windbreak and to improve the pasture.

Aylmer stored such things as rice and other staples in the ranch house. Rennie disposed of these items, deducting the price from the purchaser's pay. There were other items of which the Niihauans seemed in need. Irene talked about stocking and selling them.

Aylmer said, "Study the Hawaiians for three months. Then decide how to act toward them. But don't give them credit."

So after three months, she began supplying them with things for which they asked: Crisco, five-pound cans of coffee, canned goods, candy, clothing material.

The men wanted her to make pants for them from the denim material to wear to church. Since with only brackish water available for washing it was hard, after a single wearing, to make the pants clean again, they might quickly ask her to make another pair. She kept busy making pants, ponchos for the men to wear on horseback, "marine" hats, caring for the bees, running the store and keeping house for Rennie.

She sold clothing material to the women but did not sew their clothes. She was able to get them to do the laundry by paying them or making some trade.

As for studying the Hawaiians, Aylmer might have more accurately directed her to study the Niihauans. The aborigines were no novelty to the Haradas; they had rubbed elbows with them since childhood.

But the actions of the Haradas toward the aborigines derived more from habit and custom than from conscious reflection. A person observing them with fresh eyes might have remarked on things the Haradas took for granted.

For example, when the Christian missionaries arrived in the archipelago, early in the 19th century, they noted that the chiefs were so much larger than the common people they seemed to be of a different race. Time and the influx of foreigners wrought a change in the original stock, the aborigines interbreeding readily with the newcomers. On Niihau, though here and there one saw someone who seemed no different from the archetype, the result of this interbreeding was readily apparent. Despite the missionary observation, the aborigines, in general, were large, big-boned and muscular.

On Niihau there was daily evidence of the sturdiness of the men. Not only were all fine horsemen, they showed their physical prowess in other ways.

For example, there was Ben Kanahele (kä-nä-hā'-lĕ), who is later to loom large in this narrative. Forty-nine years old when the Harada's arrived, Ben, with his decayed and dirty teeth and unkempt appearance, looked older. But in the performance of his ranch duties, he showed youthfulness.

He would easily sling a sheep across the shoulders of his six-foot frame and carry it down to the beach to be shipped away to market. He carried to the beach, two at a time, honey cases of 130 pounds each.

In mental capacity, however, the Niihauans differed from those of aboriginal descent elsewhere. On Kauai, many with aboriginal ancestry were intelligent, educated, cultured community leaders. The schoolmaster of Niihau, Edward Kahale, had died the preceding year. Two women had replaced him, one of whom, Hannah K. Niau (nĕ-ou') figures in the story later.

Mrs. Niau had been educated in the public school at Kekaha, Kauai. In such persons who had lived away from

Niihau, the Haradas found a respectable intelligence. Those who had spent all their lives on Niihau were abysmally ignorant.

It might have seemed common charity to try to enlighten these benighted persons. But once when he found Harada trying to do so, Aylmer told him,

"Don't try to teach them anything. They're happy as they are; let them stay that way."

With Aylmer looking after them they were happy. He was like a benevolent father shielding a family of mentally retarded children from the shocks of life. The sanitary cordon he had flung around Niihau was effective; the residents tended to stay well. Though the Haradas regarded the Niihauans as slaves, they were contented slaves. They had a visible deity, Aylmer, whom they referred to as *ka haku makua,* the old lord. This deity regularly appeared to them in the flesh, bringing comfort and security.

So the uneventful days passed. The Haradas adapted. The Niihauans grew to like Harada. They encouraged him to learn and practice riding; he began to do so.

On their way home from work, some of the Niihauans would go out of their way to stop at the store to buy candy or other treats to take home. Irene bought jewelry, which she kept at the store. In 1941, in anticipation of the coming holiday season, the Haradas stocked goods appropriate to Christmas.

The Haradas had begun to look forward to the end of their third year of exile when the failing health of Rennie complicated their situation. In September 1941, feeling the need of professional medical care, the 80-year-old Rennie left for Kauai. He had not seemed seriously ill when leaving Niihau, but about three weeks later, September 28, he died in Waimea, Kauai.

The death of Rennie left Niihau without a paymaster. The Niihauans went unpaid. Persuaded of the competence and trustworthiness of Harada, Aylmer appointed him paymaster, effective the first of the year.

In the meantime, the Haradas had to cope with unpaid customers coming to the store. They accommodated the customers, who had become their friends, by violating the dictum of Aylmer to refuse credit. Harada extended credit; Irene entered the purchases in an Account Book.

On the morning Nishikaichi would land on Niihau, Irene had been giving her husband a haircut when they both noticed many Japanese planes flying north. They wondered about this phenomenon. After the great number of planes passed, they saw the planes of Nishikaichi and Ishii flying past, Ishii's plane sputtering and pouring forth black smoke.

"That one's been damaged," said Harada.

After the Haradas had eaten lunch, the two young men came galloping up and explained the situation existing near the house of Howard and the urgent need of an interpreter there.

The Haradas set off on foot for Howard's home, which was less than two miles away. Reaching their destination, they shouldered their way through the group surrounding Nishikaichi, whose forehead was bruised.

Harada addressed Nishikaichi in Japanese. "What happened to you? Where did you come from?"

Nishikaichi brightened. "Oh, you're a Japanese!"

Since the observation was a confirmation of what the local authorities had drilled into him from birth, it did not occur to Harada to protest the designation.

The pilot asked, "Can any of these people understand Japanese?"

"Perhaps a few words—no more."

The pilot regarded the couple gravely. "Don't you know Japan has attacked Pearl Harbor?"

In this way, despite having a radio, the Haradas first learned of the attack on Oahu. They had reason to fear the information might affect their standing with their neighbors; the Niihauans were as convinced of the Haradas being Japanese as the Haradas themselves. The pilot complained that when he had been unconscious, Howard had taken pistol, papers and a map of Oahu showing the position of the American fleet. The pilot wanted these articles returned to him. For the time being, the Haradas considered it prudent to keep secret what they had learned.

Still ignorant that war had broken out, the Niihauans hospitably took the pilot next door to the home of John Kelly. They plied the pilot with sweet potatoes, which he relished, and poi—a paste made of taro root—which he disliked.

They also gave him *kalua* pig—a wild pig baked in an underground oven.

The Niihauans sang, danced and played the guitar. Someone passed a guitar to the pilot. He plucked it like a samisen and sang a Japanese song.

All this time, of course, he was on the alert for a sign of the submarine that was supposed to rescue him. The submarine commander had accepted the assignment with distaste—being posted to the unrewarding task of rescuing a few strays while his compatriots could be covering themselves with glory by attacking the American Navy at Oahu. About 1:30 came a command that made him happy; he was ordered to leave the area and proceed against any ships attempting to relieve Pearl Harbor.

As time wore on, Nishikaichi had reason to believe that the rescue plan had gone awry. But as long as it was physically possible he strove to fulfill his part of the scheme.

Darkness fell. No lights showed from Kauai. The military governor had decreed an island-wide blackout. News was now coming in over the radio. It was necessary for the Niihauans, too, to blackout unless they sought destruction from the enemy and the wrath of their own side.

The Niihauans confronted the pilot. He confessed to having attacked Oahu. This time Harada considered it more prudent to interpret what the pilot said.

4

CONFINEMENT AND DELIVERANCE

Nishikaichi had not slept from the preceding day. He was wrung dry from the excitement, peril and superhuman effort of the attack on Kaneohe and Bellows and the strain of nursing his plane afterwards. They lodged him at the home of John Kelly, the Haradas remaining with him. The pilot slept as if nothing could waken him.

The Niihauans conferred on how to dispose of their unwelcome guest. Had Rennie been alive and on Niihau, he would have immediately taken charge of the situation. Rennie was gone; Harada had been appointed his successor—at least for the role of paymaster. Though Harada was compromised as being Japanese at a time when America was at war with Japan, he was, otherwise, a person of stature on Niihau.

In their insularity and ignorance, many of the Niihauans may have been unable to fully comprehend the significance of the attack. But what was clear to even the dullest was that outsiders were forbidden access to the island except through the express permission of Aylmer. Nishikaichi was not only an unapproved outsider but an enemy.

Nishikaichi had expected rescue by submarine; he had not yet completely abandoned hope. The Niihauans would be unable to prevent such a rescue. As long as they were unharmed by it, they would have considered such Japanese intervention as good riddance.

In the meantime their thoughts were on that being, Aylmer, who was accustomed to solving all hard problems for them. He was expected to arrive at Kii Landing in the morning for his weekly visit.

It was customary for some of the Niihauans to meet Aylmer on arrival. This time when they went to the rendezvous they would take Nishikaichi with them. In their naivete, they may have believed that Nishikaichi would obey Aylmer as they did. Or they may have thought that military authorities would accompany Aylmer and they could hand over Nishikaichi to them. At this time it was generally unknown in America, and on Niihau known only to the Haradas and Shintani, that a Japanese serviceman preferred death to surrender.

To go to Kii from Puuwai they would travel up a road that went along the western part of the island, the seal's back, to the nape of the seal's neck. Traversing this road would give Nishikaichi the best of opportunities to look for the missing submarine and its scout plane.

In the morning they put Nishikaichi aboard a small tractor and travelled slowly up the western side of Niihau for about seven miles. At this point the road turned eastward, across the seal's jaw, to Kii Landing, just below the seal's nostrils. There they waited for Aylmer.

He did not appear. Late in the afternoon the Niihauans returned to Puuwai.

Next day, Tuesday, the 9th, they again took the pilot to Kii. Perhaps Aylmer considered it imprudent to sail the open sea in broad daylight; they remained at Kii all night.

The sampan failing to appear, Howard, in his rough way, tried to console the pilot, whose spirits were obviously dashed.

"This island not good for you," Howard told him, "But on the other islands they have everything—doctors, everything. If you get into trouble there we will help you. We willing to help you out."

The pilot wrote, "No one can help me. Not even your God can help me."

56

The pilot and Harada walked down the beach. Out of earshot of the others they engaged in conversation.

It must have seemed to the pilot that he had fallen to a low estate, indeed. He must have compared his expectations with the reality of what had occurred from his failure to return to the carrier.

When he had been stationed at Ōmura Airfield, he had gone on a holiday, with a dozen or so buddies, to Mt. Aso in Aso National Park. As they hiked up the mountain road, filled with the vigor and promise of their youth and expectations, they had broken into the song of the *Arawashi* (Fierce Eagle) that identified them.

As they marched and sang, villagers came running, observing the flyers with deep respect. School children followed, shouting, "Banzai!" (Hurray!)

All the flyers had hoped to serve gloriously; many had done so. He had seen how Iida had chosen to die.

During the attack, Nishikaichi had been preoccupied with his own mission. Only indirectly had he marked the full result of the Japanese attack. But he had seen enough to recognize that the Japanese had scored a striking victory.

The result might have exceeded his expectations. All told the Japanese had sunk or seriously damaged 18 ships. They had plundered the Americans of the battleships *Arizona* and *Oklahoma,* the target ship *Utah* and the destroyers *Cassin* and *Downes.* They had sunk or caused to be beached the battleships *West Virginia, California* and *Nevada* and the minelayer *Oglala.* They had damaged the battleships *Tennessee, Maryland* and *Pennsylvania;* the cruisers *Helena, Honolulu* and *Raleigh,* the destroyer *Shaw,* the seaplane tender *Curtiss* and the repair ship *Vestal.*

The Japanese had destroyed 188 planes and damaged 159, killed 2403 American military personnel and wounded 1,133.

They had done all this at a loss of only 29 planes; nine Zeros, including Nishikaichi's, 15 dive bombers and five torpedo bombers.

Including Nishikaichi, the Japanese had lost 55 airmen.

They had also lost five midget submarines and their nine crewmen.

The Japanese had achieved their object of gaining a free hand in the Western Pacific. Nishikaichi had seen the superiority of the Zero to anything the Americans could put up against it. It would not do for his Zero to fall into American hands that might dissect the secrets of its superiority.

Further, as far as he knew, his were the only papers that might fall into enemy hands.

Actually American intelligence officers, some of whom were Japanese language experts, had recovered all papers, maps, orders and personal belongings from three Japanese planes and thoroughly examined them. Similar to the papers Howard had seized from Nishikaichi, they included maps of Pearl Harbor, Hickam Air Field and routine radio code instructions and other papers that might be expected in a plane sent to engage in battle. They contained nothing of value for intelligence purposes.

Yet even had Nishikaichi known his papers lacked intelligence value for the enemy, he would not have felt relieved of his responsibility towards regaining and destroying them. Death with honor included destruction of plane and papers.

Finally the Niihauans despaired of the arrival of Aylmer. They returned to Puuwai, but this time they did not stop there. Several times Harada had suggested it would be better to lodge the pilot with him; as Irene had said, "At least he would have a bed to sleep on." This time they acceded to the suggestion. They took the pilot beyond Puuwai to Kiekie.

To apprise the authorities of the delicate situation on Niihau, the Niihauans had been signaling Kauai, across the channel, from near Mt. Paniau, with six-battery flashlights. Up to this point they had treated Nishikaichi as a guest; on lodging him with Harada, they set a guard of five men over him. To ease the expense for the Haradas, the Niihauans brought fish and poi to provision the larder.

There was now ample opportunity for the Haradas to converse with the pilot. Irene asked why he had not landed his plane near the ranch house. The area was a level, grassy plain. The owner came only occasionally and was now absent.

"We have lots of gasoline here. You could have taken what you needed and flown back to your carrier."

"I thought a Caucasian might be living in this place. I didn't want to become involved with a Caucasian, so I landed far away."

Harada listened to the pilot avidly. Nishikaichi, the professional, easily imposed his judgments of the military situation on Harada, the awed amateur. Against the Japanese attack the Americans had put up such a weak defense that they seemed hopelessly incompetent. Aylmer and the American Army were expected to come to Niihau, but they did not come; very likely they were unable to come. Every night the Niihauans were using powerful flashlights to send out distress signals from Mt. Paniau; the American military took no action on the signals. The invincibility of the Japanese forces was obvious.

Also, Harada's parents were residing in Japan, in their native Fukushima. They were loyal, patriotic Japanese. What must they be thinking of the situation in Hawaii. What must they be thinking of their son and his wife, both Japanese subjects!

As the local and California, even the Federal, government had demonstrated in a hundred ways, American citizenship for the Nikkei was a technicality. Despite American citizenship, they still remained Japanese.

Though Harada was 17 years older, the 22-year-old pilot gradually gained ascendency over him. To the confused Harada, ambivalent from childhood in his attraction to Japan and America, the dedicated pilot was a steadfast guide star. The ideals of the pilot became those of Harada; the goal of death with honor so sublime that Harada came to want to help achieve it.

Harada told Irene, "If something should happen and I die, take care of things for me when I'm gone."

She had been biting her lips as she listened to the two. "Let me die with you."

Nishikaichi said, "That won't do, Mrs. Harada. Only I must die. I'll have Harada help me, but he need not die. But it might be you won't be able to live together for awhile. In any case, if the worst should happen, it's important for you to keep living in order to raise your three children. Don't commit a rash act for my sake."

Harada took care, of course, to conceal his new views from the Niihauans. But on Thursday, December 11, he took a first step in the plot by telling the Niihauans that he, as a Japanese, felt that Shintani must share the burden of responsibility for the pilot. He asked them to summon Shintani to do his share.

John Kekuhina informed Shintani of the request. Shintani begged off going that night; he would go the following day when his work would take him near Harada's house.

Friday morning, John went to Paniau to use a prearranged fire signal to indicate an emergency on Niihau.

About 7 a.m., Harada, Nishikaichi and two guards went to the apiary near Harada's home where Shintani was working. After a short conversation, the group went to Harada's home to continue the discussion.

At this point, one of the guards, Joe Kanahele, left to go fishing.

At Harada's home, Harada, Nishikaichi and Shintani spoke at length in Japanese. Shintani did not return to his duties at the apiary until shortly after 1 p.m.

About four o'clock that afternoon, a loud pounding on his door awakened Howard. He opened to admit Shintani.

Shintani was agitated. "You have paper?"

Howard, the extrovert, dug into his trophies. He showed Shintani a map of Oahu, replete with Japanese characters and with red lines converging on Pearl Harbor.

"Not that," Shintani said, "the other paper."

Howard produced papers showing sketches and photographs of American warships, papers showing radio instructions and other matters. Though unable to read the Japanese in which the papers were written, Howard assumed them to be important to the defense of America.

Shintani asked for the papers; Howard declined to part

with them. Shintani drew out about $200 in currency—a huge sum on Niihau at that time—and offered it for the papers.

"No, these papers are something important."

"You no give paper—*pilikia.*"

In the aboriginal tongue, *pilikia* (pē-lē-kē'a) means trouble. It was plain that the pilot desired the papers; Shintani was predicting evil consequences if the pilot failed to receive them.

"What kind of *pilikia*?"

"Life or *make* (mä'-kā: death)."

The threat of *make* failed to daunt Howard.

Shintani offered a compromise. "You burn paper."

Howard's patience snapped. "Get out."

Crestfallen, Shintani slunk away. So seriously did he take his prediction of *pilikia* that he straightway went into hiding in hope of averting it. But the shrinking of Shintani from the prospect of *pilikia* by no means arrested the brewing of it.

Nishikaichi and Harada recognized that they had but a weak reed to lean upon in Shintani. They went ahead with their plot without even waiting for him to report the result of his interview with Howard.

Having the key to the ranch house where shotgun and pistol were kept, Harada secretly readied the weapons, brought them out and hid them behind the door of the honey warehouse. Returning to the room occupied by Irene and Nishikaichi, Harada nodded to indicate all was ready.

In the meantime, Nishikaichi had written on a paper tape and handed the message to Irene, saying, "The Japanese Navy will soon be landing. If you have the opportunity, please report the death of Nishikaichi to the Japanese commander."

Irene glanced at the writing. It read:

Naval Airman 1st Class Shigenori Nishikaichi
Hashihama, Imabari-Iyō

She then hid the paper in a pleat of her slip.

There was only one guard, Hanaiki Niau, husband of the school teacher, on duty. Three others, evidently not taking their duties seriously, were elsewhere, ostensibly arranging work for the next day.

At about 4:30 p.m., Irene put on the hand-wound phonograph a record the Niihauans especially liked. She turned up the volume.

Nishikaichi asked permission to go to the toilet, an outhouse at the rear of the Harada home. Permission granted, the three men left, Nishikaichi leading and followed in turn by Niau and Harada. Harada made an excuse to visit the honey warehouse; the three went there.

Harada opened the door. The three entered. Harada slammed the door shut. Nishikaichi grabbed the shotgun that had been hidden behind the door. Harada fished out the revolver he had hidden under some sacks.

The conspirators pointed the guns at Niau. Harada threatened to shoot if Niau made any noise. They took Niau to the rear of the warehouse and warned him to remain there. Harada and Nishikaichi left through the front door, closing it and locking it from the outside.

Mrs. Niau, wife of the imprisoned man, had been living over the hill from the residence of the Haradas. She had been at the store to replenish supplies. Accompanied by her four children, she was returning to the village in a horse-drawn wagon. Her daughter, Loisa, was riding the horse.

Harada called to Mrs. Niau. The pilot following, Harada came running down the hill. Despite Harada's order to stop, she continued on her way.

Harada ran out, seized the horse by the bridle and brought the wagon to a stop. Pointing the shotgun at them, Harada ordered everyone but Loisa to get down from the wagon. When they obeyed, the men boarded the wagon, ordered Loisa to drive fast to Howard's home, pointing the gun at her to ensure obedience.

Loisa having departed on the horse, the insurgents left the wagon at the gate of Howard's home and arrived at the plane about 5:30 p.m. Finding the plane being guarded by 16-year-old Kalihilihi Niau, they took him into custody. With Harada prodding the youth in the back with the shotgun, they marched toward Howard's home.

Noticing Howard's only child, an eight-year-old boy in the yard, Harada asked him, "Where you father was?"

Correctly interpreting the question as an inquiry of the whereabouts of Howard, the child innocently gave misinformation. He pointed at the neighboring house. "He Kele."

Evidently believing that Howard was next door at Kelly's, the pair went to the plane and climbed on it. The pilot manipulated the radio and spoke into it.

Having parted from Shintani only five or ten minutes before, Howard had been in the outhouse when he saw Harada and the pilot approach, prodding Kalihilihi before them. He remained there. When he saw them climb on the plane, though unable to understand their actions, he saw in the movement an opportunity to escape. He burst from the outhouse and ran for cover.

"Stop! Stop!"

Unheeding, Howard raced on. Boom! the shotgun roared. The explosion inspired him to even greater speed.

He ran into the village where the people observed his agitation and gathered round him. When he told them the ordinarily peaceable, kindhearted Harada had the shotgun and had fired it at him, many refused to believe.

He warned them to evacuate the village. At the last house, he borrowed a horse.

"I'm going to Paniau to build the bonfire," he said and galloped off. But first he returned home.

While he had been gone the conspirators had ransacked his house and found the pilot's loaded pistol. Now they had a pistol they could fire. They had failed to find the papers.

Howard snatched the papers, overlooking the map of Oahu. Then he galloped to his mother-in-law's home, secreted the papers there and raced for Paniau.

In the meantime, the locked-in guard, Niau, had climbed to the second-story of the warehouse. From there he had leaped from a window to the ground. Though he cut his knee on landing in the bushes below, he ran to the village and spread the alarm. This time all the villagers believed. They fled—the women and children to spend the night in caves, in algaroba thickets and on distant beaches.

5

THE PREDICAMENT OF AYLMER

At his palatial home at Makaweli, Aylmer was fretting over the ominous portents coming from Niihau. The distress signals flashed across the channel were seen on Kauai and reported. Yet Aylmer was prevented from visiting his domain and seeing to the welfare of his vassals there.

Aylmer was an anachronism in the life of Hawaii in 1941. A resume of his antecedents gives insight into his outlook and the odd fief he maintained on Niihau.

An inbred, close-knit family, the Robinsons take interest in their genealogy. What should concern us here, however, is not their remote ancestors but those who brought about the settlement of the family in Hawaii. Also it should be of interest how they made themselves so powerful they were able to keep Niihau and its residents isolated from Hawaii and from the 20th century.

In Scotland in 1819, Capt. Francis Sinclair, 6 feet 2 inches tall and 29 years old, formerly of the Royal Navy, married Elizabeth McHutcheson. Elizabeth, born April 26, 1800 in Glasgow, was to bear him six children.

The government awarded him a grant of land in New Zealand. To New Zealand the family sailed in 1839. In 1846 he was lost at sea. In 1862 his widow sold the New Zealand estate.

In April 1863 the family sailed from New Zealand with the intention of ranching in Canada. They stopped in Hawaii en route. They arrived in Victoria in June 1863. Dissatisfied with the ranching prospects they found in that area, they again sailed for Hawaii, arriving in Honolulu September 17, 1863.

They investigated various proposals for ranching on Oahu. None pleased them. They were preparing to leave Hawaii for California when King Kamehameha IV, with whom they had become acquainted, offered them the island of Niihau for $10,000 gold.

The widow closed the deal.

There were about 600 natives on the island of Niihau at that time, none of whom knew English. At first the new ruling family dealt with the natives through an interpreter. But since it seemed essential for the newcomers to learn the language, which was then the official language of Hawaii, they learned it.

As the natives learned that all hope of their ever owning their own land had vanished with the sale of the island, they began to leave. Within two years the population had dwindled to 325. As we have seen, it was to dwindle further.

The Robinsons had brought sheep and other livestock from New Zealand. They bought more sheep, as well as cattle, in Hawaii. They established their first home on Niihau a short distance from Nonopapa, some distance inland and on a bluff.

As time wore on they began to find the isolation of Niihau oppressive. About 1869, Mrs. Sinclair concluded negotiations for rich lands at Makaweli. Settling there, she managed the affairs of the family estate until she departed this earth at the age of 92.

Her daughter Helen had married Charles Barrington Robinson, lawyer and linguist, in New Zealand in 1850. To them was born a son, Aubrey. Taking Aubrey, then one-year old, with her, Helen parted from her husband and never reunited with him.

Aubrey attended Boston University Law School and was admitted to practice in 1875. But for several years thereafter he travelled extensively in Europe and the Orient.

Returning to Hawaii, he married a first cousin, Alice

Gay. He formed a co-partnership for the cultivation of sugar with another cousin, Francis Gay. Eventually Aubrey became sole owner.

He fathered five children, of whom Aylmer was the second as well as the second son. Born at Makaweli, Aylmer, like his father, grew up to be fluent in the aboriginal language.

He attended St. Matthew's Military Academy in Burlington, California and received an AB degree from Harvard in 1910. For a year after graduation he worked at Oahu Sugar Co. in Waipahu, Oahu. In 1912, he returned to Kauai to manage the family's Makaweli ranch.

He became a partner of Gay and Robinson in 1916 and business manager of the sugar and cattle company in 1920. In 1922 he took over the management of Niihau.

He never married.

Niihau was a part of the county of Kauai. The county seat of Kauai was at Lihue, on the far side of the island from Niihau. Such was the power of Aylmer he was able to run Niihau much as he chose—without interference from county or other government.

In contrast to arid, dusty Niihau, Kauai was green and beautiful. It had been the last of the islands to submit to the rule of the conquering Kamehameha who had begun unifying the islands, in 1795, by conquering the islands of Maui, Molokai and Oahu. He had begun his conquests from his fief on the Island of Hawaii, and the name of that island followed him to typify his rule. In 1810, Kaumualii, King of Kauai, submitted to Kamehameha, and, thereupon, the residents of Kauai and Niihau, Polynesians or otherwise, became Hawaiian.

Strict Calvinist, with neither time nor inclination for frivolity, the Robinsons were respected on Kauai. But the Japanese attack on Oahu brought a swift diminution of the power of Aylmer. This quick shift in power, giving the military ascendency, is partly explainable by a provision of the Organic Act under which Hawaii was governed.

The Organic Act permitted American citizens in Hawaii to elect members of the State Legislature. The enfranchised

Aylmer Robinson, lord of Niihau, from a 1961 Honolulu Advertiser *photo. Such was the power of Aylmer, he was able to run Niihau without interference from county or other government.*

were also permitted to elect a non-voting Delegate to Congress. The U.S. President appointed the Governor.

Section 67 of the Organic Act provided that the Governor could "in case of rebellion or invasion, or imminent danger thereof, when the public safety requires it, suspend the privilege of the writ of *habeas corpus* or place the Territory, or any part thereof, under martial law until communication can be had with the president and his decision thereon made known."

Anticipation of Japanese forces landing in Hawaii was by no means limited to the opinion of Nishikaichi. The American military authorities also anticipated such an attempt and swiftly communicated this view to 72-year-old Gov. Joseph P. Poindexter.

Gov. Poindexter had reason to be shaken; during the attack a shell had fallen and exploded in the front yard of the Gubernatorial mansion, Washington Place, near the entrance. Pressured by Lieutenant General Short to declare martial law, the Governor, at 12:40 noon, the day of the attack, phoned President Roosevelt for approval. Receiving the approval, Poindexter abdicated his powers and turned over the government to the Army.

Short styled himself Military Governor, proclaimed martial law and suspended the courts along with the privilege of *habeas corpus,* that is, a writ requiring a person to be brought before a judge or court for investigation of a restraint of that person's liberty.

A scout plane from the U.S. Carrier *Enterprise* brought tangible evidence of the Oahu attack to Kauai. The pilot had been ordered to land on Ford Island, Pearl Harbor. Arriving there he found it under attack. He tried to return to his carrier but was unable to find it. He landed in a pasture on Kauai in such a state of shock he was sent to Waimea Hospital.

The Army mobilized; Kauai became an armed camp.

In these circumstances, Aylmer was the more concerned about the situation on Niihau. But the iron might of military rule frustrated him. The Navy decreed that no boats might leave port until all fishing sampans at sea during the attack on Oahu were located and accounted for. Aylmer pleaded his anxiety for his people and pleaded in vain.

His anxiety increased as the distress signals beamed from near Mt. Paniau were reported by sentries patrolling the Kauai shore of the Kaulakahi Channel. Then came the symbol of desperation—a bonfire, the first ever. But his pleading to be permitted to visit his Niihau domain fell on deaf ears.

He was stewing in anxiety on Saturday morning when he received a phone call. To the amazement of Aylmer, the caller identified himself as Howard.

"*Pilikia,*" Howard told him.

"Where are you?"

"Down Waimea Police Station."

"I'll be there," said Aylmer.

Aylmer hurried. When he reached Waimea, he found that not only Howard but five other Niihauans were in Waimea. Howard briefed Aylmer on the developments on Niihau and explained his presence in Waimea.

About 9 p.m., the preceding night, when Howard had reached a point between Paniau and Koolaukani Valley, he found some men there trying to signal Kauai with kerosene lamps and reflectors. They set the signal fire. But they decided the situation was too extreme to rely on the signal fire alone to bring them aid.

With five others, Howard descended to Kii. With Kekuhina Kohelaulii as captain, they pushed off in a lifeboat and began to row towards Kauai. It was then about 12:30 p.m. There was a gallon of water in the boat but no food. As they drew out to sea they faced the dismal prospect of bucking headwinds all the way across.

Since they might be mistaken for an enemy boat, they ran the risk of attack by navy planes.

As they drew away from land, some wanted to return to see to the safety of their families.

Howard told them, "You can't see your families now. They all in the bush. Cannot. Gotta get help."

The moon had passed its last quarter. The stars were brilliant. At their backs as they rowed against the rough sea, the wind blew the foam from the wave tops against them. As each man drew on his oar, he could see Venus high in the western sky and the constellation of Orion to the east.

After three hours, they saw fire rising from Puuwai from about the neighborhood of Howard's house. Had the Niihauans overpowered the insurgents and set fire to the plane? What reason would they have for putting the torch to the plane?

They rowed and rowed while their hands blistered and their backs ached, one man relieving another when the strength of the first gave out. The changes in the position of the stars showed them the passage of time. At 6:30 a.m. light began to glimmer beyond the northernmost of the island they had left.

Day broke upon them and, with daybreak, the danger of being seen and attacked by a Navy patrol plane. But for three and a half hours they rowed in broad daylight without mishap.

At 10:30 a.m. they reached the village of Waimea. People were congregated on the landing. Many of them had been civilians less than a week before, but now they were armed with shotguns and 30-30 rifles.

One pointed to a sign that said: Boats Not Allowed to Enter. "Hey, you no see that sign?"

Howard replied, "Well, dat you speak to Robinson. This is Robinson's boat." For it was inconceivable to him that, even with a war on, anyone might challenge the authority of Robinson.

The sentry continued, "Why should you row a boat? You like dat? No plenty *kaukau* (food). You still spend time in that? You still have plenty food? You don't know that Pearl Harbor was bombed by the Japanese?"

Worldly wise beyond his companions, Howard told them, "Stay in the boat. Don't tell nobody what was the trouble at Niihau till I come back."

At this point, two policemen approached. One of them said to Howard, "I want to talk to you." They took him into custody, but more in the manner of being helpful than if they suspected him of any wrongdoing.

When they arrived at the police headquarters, Howard asked, "May I speak to Robinson on the phone?"

They gave permission. He put through the call. Aylmer arrived promptly.

Speaking in English, with the police listening, Howard gave the events of the past week on Niihau to Aylmer. The curious gathered around to listen.

A policeman went out with Aylmer's foreman to gather the rest of the lifeboat crew.

Aylmer asked Howard, "Did you eat?"

"No, we all hungry. But we had water."

Aylmer took them to a Chinese restaurant and fed them. Then they went to Barking Sands to tell the military.

So ended the first step of their hazardous journey in search of aid. They were at leisure to reflect on the families they had left behind and to wonder if even Aylmer could reach them in time to succor them.

6

MIZUHA SEEKS VINDICATION

When the shocked American pilot landed on Kauai, 1st. Lt. Jack Mizuha (mē-zōō-hä), 28, was in full command at Burns field, Hanapepe, the principal airport of the island. Next day the Army reduced him to executive officer.

The reduction in rank when the military was in acute need of competent officers, and in the face of his proven competence and dedication, apparently grew out of peculiarities in his background. So at this point an analysis of these peculiarities as they relate to him and to the Niihau Incident, as the events occurring on Niihau would come to be called, is appropriate.

He had been born November 5, 1913 in the village of Waihee, Island of Maui, to Genzaburō and Nami Mizuha. According to Jack, Genzaburō, born in 1860 in Hiroshima Prefecture, Japan, had first come to Hawaii in 1882, at a time when there were only a handful of Japanese in the Islands. Thereafter he made several trips back to Japan. Genzaburō was of the samurai class and well-educated; he spoke English. After running a hotel in Honolulu he came to Maui to build irrigation tunnels for Wailuku Sugar Co.

Nami was Genzaburō's third wife and not of the samurai class. She was a picture bride. That is, according to the Japanese custom of the period, the prospective bride, in Japan, and the prospective groom, in Hawaii, through a matchmaker, had exchanged photographs and personal information. Then, at the expense of the groom, the bride had been dispatched to Hawaii. There the betrothed met for the first time and straightway became man and wife.

By this marriage, Jack became the third child and second son; there would be a younger brother. By combining three Chinese characters meaning *Japan-Hawaii-son,* the father named this third child Hifuo. He would be known only by the name of Hifuo until he reached the sixth grade of primary school.

Invoking the power the educators of the time seemed to possess, the primary school principal conferred on Hifuo the name Jack.

Mizuha went through the usual procedure for children of Japanese immigrants of making a formal effort to acquire something of the ancestral tongue. But though he completed Japanese language school through the eighth grade, he was unproficient in the language.

After being educated in the public schools of Maui, he matriculated at the University of Hawaii. At the University he took the advanced Reserve Officers Training Corps instruction offered to those students interested in obtaining a reserve commission in the Army. Upon graduation, he became a 2nd lieutenant in the Reserve.

He learned shorthand and served as police patrolman clerk from 1934 to 1936. In the meantime continuing his studies, he earned a master's degree in education from the University of Hawaii in 1936.

Born a dual citizen, Mizuha, March 28, 1936, divested himself of his Japanese citizenship in formal expatriation proceedings in which he declared his desire to sever ties to his father's country of birth. The same year he went to Kauai and became a teacher in Waimea High School.

In May 1941, in a discussion in the 11th grade social studies class, he predicted war with Japan. Before the year was over, before the class graduated, it might experience the reality of modern war.

"Bombs might fall on Waimea," he said.

A portent of what such a conflict might mean to him occurred at the plantation theater in the present town of

Kaumakani, at that time called Makaweli, to which he escorted a young lady. He tried to buy a ticket in the reserved section. The management refused to sell; the section was reserved for Caucasians.

In the summer of 1941, he was appointed principal of Huleia School, Kauai. He had married in 1936. A daughter had been born to him in 1938. Now he moved his family and belongings to this village, five miles from Lihue.

August 31, 1941, he received an order to report for active military service at Fort Shafter, Oahu. He left for Fort Shafter September 9, having served only six days as principal.

At Tripler General Hospital, Honolulu, physicians found him physically qualified for service. The Army ordered him back to Kauai to serve with the 299th Infantry at Hanapepe.

At Hanapepe he became absorbed in Army life. His superiors placed him in command of Burns Field.

As a Nikkei, Mizuha had been subjected to the same official indoctrination as Harada. The authorities had registered him in the public schools as of Japanese nationality. Despite his expatriation, he was still officially identified as Japanese.

Always having confounded the Nikkei with the Japanese, the newspapers bent to the theme with increased zeal. Of the 40 or so shells that had fallen on Honolulu during the attack, including the one that fell on the Governor's doorstep, 39 were anti-aircraft shells. The addled defenders had failed to set the fuses to these; so instead of exploding among the enemy planes, the shells had exploded on impact with the ground, maiming and killing Honolulu residents, most of whom were Nikkei. The newspapers hinted at condign justice in so many "Japanese bombs" killing so many Japanese.

While the attack was still in progress, the FBI was rounding up Japanese suspected of being potentially dangerous. These included enemy alien businessmen, religious and community leaders, officers of Japanese associations, Shintō and Buddhist priests and priestesses, Japanese-language

Jack Mizuha. As 1st Lt. Mizuha, he was executive officer of Burns Field, Kauai, when he received the calamitous news of what was occurring on Niihau.

newspaper editors and owners and Japanese-language school officials or teachers.

Nikkei still at large, even though locally born and educated, were subjected to official scrutiny. The military was everywhere—behind sandbags on downtown Honolulu street corners, in the public parks, along the beaches.

Nikkei were permitted to work in some of these off-limit areas. But they worked like prisoners of war, with armed guards standing over them and even accompanying them to the latrine.

As we have seen, the anti-Nikkei sentiment brought a swift demotion to Mizuha. But until the landing at Waimea of the lifeboat from Niihau, he might have been comforted by the thought that the charges against the Nikkei were based only on gossip and rumor. The report of Howard, however, indicated that, from the Nikkei point of view, the worst had happened: aided by a Nisei, an enemy pilot was terrorizing Niihau.

Mizuha had his work quarters in the orderly room in one wing of the two-story, blacked-out wooden barracks. There was a desk and typewriter for him and a desk for the commanding officer.

He was sitting in this room just before noon when the report of events on Niihau reached him. Far from being dismayed, he found the report offered him opportunity.

He picked up the phone and called Lt. Col. Eugene J. Fitzgerald, commander of the Kauai District. Mizuha volunteered to lead a rescue squad to Niihau. In support of his offer, he marshalled arguments.

The commanding officer was expected to lead the squad but Mizuha was younger. Mizuha was one of the first reservists recalled to duty. He had kept up his studies. While teaching at Waimea High School he had done extra work for the Army.

He flung down a challenge. Fitzgerald had always insisted upon the loyalty of the Nikkei. Here was the opportunity to demonstrate his sincerity by appointing Mizuha leader of the rescue squad.

For three days the Robinson family had been besieging

Fitzgerald with requests to send a boat to Niihau. Since the Navy had ordered all boats off the water, he had been unable to accede. Now that he was authorized to form an expedition to relieve Niihau, he had reason to believe that the choice of Mizuha to lead it would be unpopular.

With the war less than a week old, the Japanese had been carrying everything before them. On the same day they had attacked Oahu they had landed forces at Singora and Patani in Thailand and at Kota Bahru, Malaya. The next day they attacked Hong Kong and destroyed 100 enemy aircraft in the Philippines. December 10, they landed in the N. Philippines, captured the American island of Guam and the British islands of Tarawa and Makin besides sinking the British battleship *Prince of Wales* and the British cruiser *Repulse*. December 11 they attacked Wake.

Press and radio continued to identify the Nikkei with the enemy. The draft status of the Nikkei was changed to 4-c enemy alien, making them undraftable and unacceptable. At Schofield Barracks, 1,564 Nikkei soldiers were stripped of their weapons and demoted to a work detail. January 19, 1942, the Territorial Guard of Hawaii would brusquely dismiss its Nikkei members.

Nervous sentries stood on the street corners of Honolulu. In the darkness of the blacked-out night, if a pedestrian ignored a command to halt, whether from heedlessness or deafness, he invited death.

In this situation, though doubtless sorely tried by the information from Niihau, the faith of Fitzgerald held firm. He directed Mizuha to lead the rescue squad.

Hoping to pick the best men available, mature men about his own age, Mizuha called for volunteers. Among those who responded was another Nikkei, Ben Kobayashi (kō-bä-yä'shē).

The parents of Kobayashi had come from Hiroshima, Japan, as contract laborers. Ben was born to them on Kauai January 16, 1911, third in a family that would amount to four boys and four girls. He had attended Japanese language school but, failing to apply himself, had learned little there.

Nevertheless, through daily use, he had learned to speak Japanese fluently.

Kobayashi had become acquainted with Harada when both had been stevedoring at Port Allen, Kauai. After Harada had given up stevedoring to drive the oil truck, the acquaintance had sufficiently continued for an exchange of greetings on meeting. But when Kobayashi learned of the situation on Niihau, it did not occur to him that the Nisei aiding the pilot was his former co-worker Harada.

Kobayashi had volunteered for the National Guard December 10, 1940, a little more than a month before his 30th birthday. He had been discharged November 10, 1941 but had been recalled immediately after the Japanese attack on Oahu. On patrol and sentry duty at night he had seen and wondered at the signal-like flashes emanating from Niihau.

Long wanting to visit Niihau, like most others he had been barred from doing so. He had served as driver for Mizuha and had thus learned of his unproficiency in Japanese.

Kobayashi said, "Hey, let me go! I'll be the translator."

Mizuha accepted the offer, though cautioning that each man would be required to do whatever might be necessary for the success of the mission.

Navy and Army co-operated to make the trip possible. The former Inter-Island ship, the *S.S. Kukui,* now a lighthouse tender, had come to Waimea that day after making its rounds putting out lights. A little after 6 p.m., when darkness had fallen, Mizuha, 13 enlisted men, the six Niihauans, Aylmer and Port Allen Harbormaster Eugene L. McManus sailed on her from Waimea.

During the trip, Aylmer and Mizuha, with their divergent views and aims may have acted abrasively on each other. Aylmer stressed that the Niihauans were a religious people. He wanted to avoid bloodshed. Taking his men in what he perceived as a combat situation, Mizuha may have been more concerned about their becoming the victims of bloodshed.

The Kauai Radio Broadcasting had heightened this concern by blunderingly broadcasting that a rescue party was on its way to Niihau. Since there were two radios on Niihau, the enemy might have picked up the report and prepared to ambush the rescuers.

Aylmer counseled the Niihauans, "Don't make any false moves or try to make trouble."

Howard reassured him. "We don't want to make trouble."

Going on their first combat mission, the soldiers were too tense to talk much.

The sky was clear and glittering with stars, but rough seas prevented them from landing on Niihau. Until daybreak Sunday the *Kukui* patrolled back and forth along the southern tip of the island. Then the rescue squad prepared to land at a cove there, Nanopuka, between Leahi and Kaumuhonu Bay.

About 7:30 a.m. they got into the lighter; crew members rowed them to shallow water. They leaped from the lighter and waded ashore.

They breakfasted on sandwiches, bread and milk and set out for Puuwai.

To avoid presenting a target to the terrorists, the platoon advanced in combat formation, the men spaced from five to ten yards apart. On each flank, about 40 yards ahead, an experienced scout explored each suspicious place. Rifle at the ready, he might circle what appeared to be a deserted shack. Satisfied that no enemy lurked there, he would signal the following soldiers that all was clear.

With Aylmer following, they marched up the western side of Niihau. They turned right at Nonopapa, crossed the pasture and, bypassing Kiekie, turned north towards Puuwai.

About 1:30 p.m., after a 14-mile march, they began to sneak up on the village. Just as they reached the hill on the crest of which is the village, they heard the church bell toll. The soldiers exchanged glances. Church services with two terrorists at large!

Mizuha shouted, "Close ranks!"

The men closed ranks and marched over the hill.

7

THE END AND AFTERMATH
OF THE INSURGENCY

As the Niihauans had pulled out to sea in the lifeboat, the situation on Niihau had taken a turn for the worse. Finding Howard gone, most of the papers missing and the village deserted, the insurgents became enraged. They captured Kalanapio Niau and ordered him to summon the others. With the guns in his back, Niau responded by going through the village calling.

Kaahakila Kalimahuluhulu—called Kalima, for short— heard the call. Thinking the call was for help, he went out to the road to lend assistance. The insurgents seized him.

The insurgents tied Kalima's hands behind him. The group went through the village calling. No one else responded.

The group returned to the plane. The insurgents had piled the machine gun cartridges on the wing. Nishikaichi again went to the plane radio, put on the earphones and began talking. The captives heard no reply.

The insurgents now directed Niau to carry the cartridges to the wagon, still at the gate. Harada remarked there were enough cartridges to kill every man, woman and child on Niihau.

When Niau returned to the plane, he found the insurgents had removed the machine guns. They forced Niau to carry the guns to the wagon.

Night had fallen and the enterprise was failing to prosper. Harada told Kalima to go to Kiekie and tell Irene her husband would not be home that night—he would be looking for Howard.

Kalima made a pretense of obeying the order. But when he felt he had reached a safe distance, he turned away from Kiekie and headed for the beach. There he found his wife and had her untie his hands.

He also discovered the aforementioned Ben Kanahele. Kalima conspired with Ben to sneak back to the plane to steal the machine guns and ammunition.

While Kalima and Ben put their heads together on this project, the insurgents wandered through the dark, deserted village, shooting off their guns and calling upon Howard to give himself up. They seized such Niihauans as they discovered, keeping some as hostages while sending others to search for Howard.

They also searched those houses that seemed likely repositories for the missing papers. They wandered into the home of Mrs. Huluwani and found her seated in a rocking chair, reading her Bible by lamp light. Because she was unable to walk, she had not fled with the others.

Harada demanded the whereabouts of Howard. She continued her reading.

"Shall I shoot her?" Harada asked.

She said calmly, *"Ke Akua ke hiki ke pepehi."* (Only God can kill.) She went on with her reading.

He fired the shotgun into the ceiling. But she remained unmoved, they went on their way.

They had taken the machine guns from the wagon and into the village. Now they went back to the wagon and found the ammunition gone. Kalima and Ben had stolen it and hidden it on the beach.

On the theory that if the papers were secreted in Howard's house flames would destroy them, about 3 a.m. the insurgents set it ablaze. They poured gasoline over the plane and set it afire, but only succeeded in burning out the cockpit and damaging the fuselage.

After fasting from the preceding afternoon, the refugees

had grown hungry. Ben, his wife, Ella and Kalima's wife tried to sneak back into the village to get food. The insurgents captured them.

The insurgents told them that if Howard would be returned the villagers would be safe. If he were not returned, the insurgents would kill all the villagers.

Despite the inconsistency, they also threatened to kill the two women and then kill themselves. Instead, they sent Kalima's wife to look for Howard. She pretended to do so until sufficiently distant from them to escape.

Then the insurgents directed Ben to look for Howard. They kept Ella as hostage.

Ben knew Howard had left for Kauai. But Ben went into the thickets calling for Howard by the name by which he was known on Niihau, "Hawila! Hawila!"

Soon concern for the safety of Ella caused him to abandon his game of make believe. He returned to her.

The pilot realized he was being tricked. Harada said, "If you don't find Howard, the pilot will kill you and all the people of the village."

They were standing on a boulder-strewn incline, near a stone wall. The pilot held the shotgun, his pistol stuck in his boot top. Harada was carrying extra shotgun cartridges.

The Niihauans were loyal to each other. And all were threatened with death—Ben, Ella, Ben's five brothers, his sister, his two daughters and all the others.

In the aboriginal tongue, Ben said, "Take the pistol away from him before he kills someone."

"If I try to do that, he will kill me, too."

But it was not fear of death that deterred Harada. When he had started out to help regain the papers and burn the plane, he may have meant to do no more harm to the natives than ruffling their feelings. But as time wore on and success had eluded him, he had become more involved. He had fired at some. He had helped burn down the home of a friend and neighbor. He had made himself an outcast, the villagers solidly arrayed against him.

Forsaken, guilty of terrorism, kidnapping, arson and the more heinous crime of giving aid and comfort to the enemy in time of war, he shrank from what the future might hold for him. Capture would mean imprisonment, merciless grilling and, at the end, probable execution. By his actions he had imperilled his family. Alive he imposed a greater threat to their safety than he would if dead.

Further, there were the ties to America he had broken. Japanese culture decreed he might atone for this apostasy, at least in part, through symbolical apology. He unbuttoned his shirt as if preparing to commit ritual suicide.

Ben narrowly observed the fatigue and discouragement of his opponents. The desperate situation lent him desperate courage.

Harada gave the extra cartridges to the pilot and reached for the shotgun. As the pilot surrendered the shotgun and turned away, Ben and Ella leaped at him.

The pilot jerked the pistol from his boot top. Ella grabbed his arm and brought it down. The pilot shouted an order to Harada. Harada pried Ella loose. The pilot fired three times, wounding Ben in the left chest, left hip and penis.

Using the same grip he used in handling sheep, Ben picked up the pilot by neck and leg and dashed him against the stone wall. The pilot fell stunned. Ella leaped at him and beat in his head with a rock. Drawing his hunting knife, the wounded Ben cut Nishikaichi's throat.

"I was so mad!" he explained later, "I was so mad!"

Unconditioned to such violence, Harada was shaken. He looked at the corpse of the man to whom he had looked for leadership and support. He despaired.

He put shells in the shotgun and turned it on himself. His first shot went wild. He pressed the muzzle against his belly and pulled the trigger again; the shot entered his vitals.

Observing the dead pilot, the dying Harada, her wounded husband; recoiling from the experience of beating in a man's head, the terrified Ella gathered up pistol and shotgun and ran for help. In her flight she dropped the weapons and was never able to remember where.

Some five years later a flood would flush the shotgun out beside the stone wall. There it would remain until some natives, clearing the brush, would find it. They would conclude that the pistol must also be near by, but they would never find it.

After Ella left, Ben began to stagger away.

"Help me," Harada said, "Don't leave me here to die alone."

"I'm in trouble, too," said Ben, "I'm either going to die here with you or on the way home."

He chose home and reached there.

———

Howard, as guide, had seen a portent of what awaited the rescue party. As they had approached the village, he had noticed tethered horses grazing. He had turned to the soldier accompanying him.

"Look at the horses; still tied yet."

Since the soldier seemed unable to recognize the significance of the tethered horses, Howard added, *"Pilikia all pau."* (The trouble is over.)

But needing further assurance and being near the home of his brother-in-law, Joe Kanahele, Howard rushed in. He found his two nephews, Henry, 16, and Isaac, 12, asleep. He woke them.

"Hey," he demanded, "where the Japanee? Where the Japanee?"

"Make," his startled nephews told him, "The Japanee *make* already."

Spying the soldiers from the church, the congregation rushed out, at first fearfully, believing the Japanese army had come to wreak vengeance. As they recognized their own men, their fear turned to joy. They ran towards them, calling out in their own language.

Mabel Kaleohano rushed to Howard and threw her arms around him. "Oh, Papa," she wept, "we lost our house."

"Never mind the house. I'm glad you didn't lose your life. We don't give a damn about the house."

Aylmer quickly came from behind the soldiers, calling to the Niihauans in the same language they were using. At the

84

sound of his voice, the Niihauans fell into respectful silence. They answered his questions.

Aylmer told the soldiers that the pilot and Harada were dead. The platoon assembled at the schoolhouse.

In the schoolhouse, Mizuha held a hearing on the events of the past week. Mrs. Hannah K. Niau, schoolteacher and principal, officiated with Aylmer interpreting. Descendent of two generations of lawyers, Aylmer was not only the interpreter for his charges but their advocate. He repeated nothing that might bring suspicion or trouble on them. Mizuha took notes in shorthand.

The hearing over, the Niihauans led the platoon to where the bodies lay, about 100 yards distant. There in the heat the soldiers found the two—Harada in a fetal position, his shirt drawn tightly over his bloated belly; Nishikaichi lying on his side. Rats or feral cats had eaten Nishikaichi's eyeballs. Much of his face had been gnawed away; what remained swarmed with maggots and flies. The bodies stank.

Medics of the platoon stripped the pilot of his clothing. Mizuha took notes and ordered burial of the corpses.

Near the schoolhouse, the Niihauans served a lunch of fried fish and rice for the soldiers. Flies swarmed to share the food.

Howard led a group to fetch Shintani. Despite his relief over finding his wife safe, Howard was in an unforgiving mood. He called to Shintani that they had come for him.

Shintani and his wife came to the door. His wife wept.

"My husband never do nothing," she protested.

"He only told me *pilikia;* he didn't tell me the pilot was coming. Why didn't he tell me?"

Without waiting for explanation, he crossed Shintani's wrists and tied them with rope. Before the assembled villagers, they marched Shintani to the schoolhouse and tied his hands behind the flagpole on the steps.

The humiliation of Shintani found expression in an attack of asthma.

Seeing the prisoner pale and strangling, Kobayashi told him in Japanese. "These guys are nuts, but it's war. I'm only a private first class, so though I want to help you I can't do much.''

Nevertheless, he persuaded a Niihauan to bring medicine from Shintani's home to ease the asthma.

Shintani appealed to Aylmer about the bound hands. "It's very painful." He asked to be unbound.

In the same language, Aylmer said, "Ask the lieutenant."

Acting on his own suggestion, Aylmer turned to Mizuha, "Can you release this man?"

Mizuha ordered Shintani unbound.

After getting the story from the Niihauans, Aylmer and the soldiers went to Kiekie to get Irene.

During the terror, some Niihauans had come to the Harada home and asked Irene to try to pacify her husband.

She had told them, "How can I, a woman, face bullets when you can't?"

This insult to their manhood was contrary to what they wanted of her. They had turned away in such anger she feared for her safety.

Having the keys to the ranch house, she entered with Taeko and locked herself in. She theorized that however great might be their desire to wreak vengeance on her, the Niihauans would not harm the property of Aylmer.

In the morning, a loyal friend of Harada, a brother of Ben, had come and told her, with tears in his eyes, that Harada and Nishikaichi were dead. She assumed both had committed suicide. But burdened with a small child, she feared to go to the distant place where the bodies were said to lie. Instead she cowered in her home as Aylmer and the rescue squad came for her.

The sun was setting when they reached her home where they found her sobbing. Aylmer, pale and shaking with rage, confronted her.

He ordered, "Be ready to leave in ten minutes."

Inside the blacked-out house it was already growing dark. She pointed to her stock of goods, jewelry and Christmas merchandise. "What about my things? Where is Harada?"

86

"Harada will be leaving on Monday. He'll pack all these things and bring them."

She had been told that Harada was dead. Aylmer had seen the bloated corpse. The words of Aylmer further confused her; she seemed to be living in a world where truth was falsehood and falsehood truth.

It seemed plain, however, that nothing was to be gained through further appeals to her enraged employer. She gathered together what she could; it was necessary to leave most of her belongings behind. In her haste, because of the blackout and because of her concern for Taeko, she forgot some jewelry and the Account Book in which she kept the record of credit extended.

The Niihauans harnessed the tractor to a wagon. Ella came with Ben, wounded but still able to walk. With the pilot's clothes and papers, except for the map destroyed in the fire at Howard's home, all boarded the wagon. About 9 p.m. they arrived at Nonopuka where the *Kukui* was waiting.

Kobayashi wanted to assist Irene. It was not only that she was the widow of the man he had known favorably. She and he were of similar background, born on the island of Kauai, molded in similar circumstances, second-class citizens under a local government American in name but alien in spirit. He carried Taeko across the rocks to the lighter that would take them to the *Kukui*.

On the *Kukui* the soldiers tied Shintani to a stanchion. When Kobayashi approached, Shintani asked, "Why do you have me tied up like this?"

"So you won't commit suicide."

"Why should I commit suicide! I have a family on Niihau."

They left Irene free to roam the deck with her child. Like Shintani, she was drawn to Kobayashi, the member of the rescue squad who seemed to best understand the prisoners and to be most kindly disposed towards them. Still all the soldiers pitied her, though the only testimony they had heard had been a justification of the actions of the Niihauans and a condemnation of the Haradas.

Still uncertain of what had befallen her husband, hoping

against hope that he might still be alive, she asked Kobayashi, "Where's Harada?"

Mizuha had told the rescue squad it was not their duty to question the prisoners. To spare her, Kobayashi said, "Harada's been taken to Honolulu."

Each time she approached him with the same question, he gave her the same answer.

Irene might have expected sympathy from Shintani as a fellow sufferer. Instead he upbraided her.

"Why didn't you control your husband?"

Again she stabbed at masculine pride. "How could I control him—I, a woman—when you, a man, could not?"

This taunt had the anticipated effect.

He reflected on his life on Niihau and on the family he had left there. All had been serene until Nishikaichi had come with convincing arguments of the invincibility of Japan.

The arguments had conjured up the specter of Japan lodging treason charges against Shintani and his family if he failed to assist the pilot. So Shintani had permitted himself to be inveigled into trying to buy the pilot's papers from Howard.

Though he had failed in the mission, Shintani was now tied up like a dangerous beast, disgraced among his family, relatives and friends—being sent into exile, perhaps to execution.

8

THE ORDEAL OF IRENE

They arrived at Port Allen, Kauai at 7:30 a.m., Monday, December 15. An Army detail was on hand to take possession of the wounded and the prisoners. Ben being the only wounded, they put him and Ella in an ambulance and transported them to Waimea Hospital. There, at 8:10 a.m., the soldiers carried the Niihauan on a stretcher into the hospital.

Dr. Burt O. Wade, who attended Ben, found the wounds superficial. Ben would make a complete recovery.

Colonel Fitzgerald hustled Mizuha off to Command Headquarters in Lihue.

The Army transported Irene and Shintani to Waimea Jail, casting them into cells across from each other. Accustomed to disfavor under American law, and now an enemy alien, Shintani had reason to expect the worst. But he must have been surprised that neither the sex of Irene nor her American citizenship brought her better treatment than that accorded him.

First they took Taeko away from her. Taeko would be delivered into the hands of Haruyo, the older sister already caring for two Harada children.

Shintani was free to scrutinize the bereaved wife and dispossessed mother at leisure, for she had no more privacy than a caged animal. The two shared the same shower and toilet. Armed guards kept her under surveillance 24 hours a day, the guard being kept alert by being changed every two hours. All her necessary functions were observed by the guard as well as by Shintani.

Dr. Tadao Hata, 36, who had been practicing medicine on Kauai since 1932, and who had delivered two of Irene's three children, came to the Waimea Jail.

Shintani railed, "I was happy. Why did Japan have to come and do this?"

The chief object of his resentment seemed not Japan but Harada. At the widow, Shintani continued to direct the bitter reproach, "Because of your husband, I'm here."

His complaint evoked no sympathy. She lay on her cot in a stupor of despair. For five days she refused the food they brought her.

She left the cell only when two guards came, handcuffed her and, with fixed bayonets, led her to be interrogated.

The authorities suspected her of being a spy and went to great lengths to force her to talk. But the vile treatment they were according her increased her fierce resistance. Though they could charge her with betraying her country, they would find no justification for charging her with disloyalty to her husband. She was, nevertheless, careful to obliquely absolve herself of involvement in the incident and of any responsibility for it.

She would tell her questioners. "He had everything to live for, but he gave up his life. Could he do more than that?"

She refused to identify the pilot by name. They searched her clothing, but the note Nishikaichi had given her had become lost. They pried off the soles and heels of her shoes looking for information. Finding nothing, they doused all the clothing she had worn to jail with kerosene and burned them.

Some matters of military value related to the flight of Nishikaichi had been available and disregarded. Before the attack an Army radar station at Kahuku Point, Oahu, had tracked an unusually large number of approaching planes and been told to disregard the finding. After the attack, while the defenders sought the attacking fleet to the south, the same radar station tracked the Japanese planes flying north. No one thought to ask the radar station for information.

When all the clues available are considered, it might seem odd that the Army never learned the identity of the pilot. The reason for the failure can be found in the situation in America before the attack. The American authorities tended to be ignorant of Japan, ignorant of the Japanese and ignorant of the Japanese language.

Lt. Col. Kendall J. Fielder, chief intelligence officer for the U.S. Army, Pacific, had Japanese language experts on his staff. But the number of such experts available to the military were far too few for the mountain of work that needed to be done.

The unbending attitude of Irene averted official sympathy, but her refusal to eat aroused alarm. The keepers brought a minister to console her and to attempt to awaken a desire to survive.

The Army transferred her to the Kauai County Jail at Wailua. Later they sent her to Sand Island, Honolulu, and then to Honouliuli, near Waipahu, Oahu.

They sent Shintani, the enemy alien, to mainland internment. But because she, being an American citizen, might have been freed on a writ of *habeas corpus* had she been sent there, they kept her in Hawaii.

At Honouliuli, the few women prisoners were housed in two one-story frame buildings surrounded by barbed wire. They were segregated from the far more numerous men, some of whom had achieved notoriety. From a distance, she sometimes saw Ensign Kazuo Sakamaki, commander of a Japanese midget submarine, who had been taken prisoner the morning after the attack. Sometimes she saw the German spy, Bernard Julius Otto Kuehn, being taken for questioning; she heard him being beaten.

Confined with her was Kuehn's wife, Friedel, and his stepdaughter, Ruth, said to have been a mistress of the German Minister of Propaganda Josef Goebbels. Friedel, and the other German women as well, seemed always to be fighting for their rights, sometimes successfully.

On a visit to Japan, the Kuehns had lodged at the Imperial Hotel in Tokyo. Friedel used to tell Irene, "After the war you should open a shop in the Imperial Hotel."

The Italian women did not fight back at their captors; the Japanese women simply did what they were told. But when a letter came telling all the women they were to remain interned for the duration of the war, the German and Italian women wept loudly. The Japanese women did not weep.

The husband of the matron was a former customs official, accustomed to searching luggage and examining the faces of persons.

"He was a mean one."

The men prisoners pitied the women and asked if they could do anything for them. The women pointed out that they had neither tables nor chairs. The men built these articles for the women.

During her long confinement, whenever something might turn up to attract official attention to her, guards would take her, in handcuffs, to be questioned by the FBI. Sometimes one FBI agent would question her, sometimes two, sometimes three.

They would ask if she had been a spy. She would answer negatively. They would ask about her trip to Japan and inquire if she wanted to visit Japan again. She would say she had enjoyed her trip and might enjoy another trip.

"I think Japan is a nice place to visit."

An agent put a map of Japan against a blackboard and asked, "Don't you think you'd like to see Japan wiped off the map?"

During the war, the FBI, under Robert Shivers, was a moderating influence on the general hysteria. Because of the objectivity of the agency, the Nikkei fared much better than they might have otherwise. So perhaps there was method in the apparent madness of the agent in pursuing such an asinine line of questioning. Perhaps he believed that his achieving this height of asinity would so disgust her that she might respond in anger and without restraint. If so, he must have been disappointed.

"I'm not a politician. I've never thought about it."

92

She had no information of military value to impart, though the keen interest of the agents might have encouraged her to believe she had. Her refusal to talk derived from the brusque condemnation of Aylmer, the vile treatment the Army had accorded her at Waimea and, while she still felt he might be alive, the fear that talking of the incident might incriminate Harada further. She also had reason to believe that giving the full details of the Incident, far from ameliorating her situation, would render it worse.

Then from her torment had burst a revelation. Had she talked freely, the authorities would have quickly lost interest in her. Her refusal to talk presented them with a mystery and a challenge. They could not neglect her.

Since her interrogators set such store on the information she had, she came to esteem it in equal measure. She fed her self-esteem on this conclusion. Here were these skilled agents of a mighty nation—men who had received the advantages and preferment denied her. When she faced them, they became impotent. They could imprison her; they could not break her.

At the price of martyrdom she had bought her secrets. She came to cherish them, gloating over them like a miser counting his treasure coin by coin. Ordeal and riches, torment and joy became intertwined, grew into a unity on which to base behavior.

In the boredom and idleness of her internment, she found other subjects to invite reflection. One such was the pilot who was the cause of her ordeal. She might have found it of interest had she known how his family mourned him.

Immediately after the Oahu attack, since Nishikaichi failed to return to his carrier, the Japanese navy informed his family that he had been killed in action. The navy posthumously promoted him two grades to special duty ensign.

Accepting neighborly congratulations for his heroism, the family mourned him. His mother, to whom he had been close, had occasion to recollect many occasions on which he had shown concern or tenderness toward her.

When he had been a middle school student, she had often awakened in the morning to the sound of his footsteps coming down the stair. She would follow him. He would be in the kitchen, standing before the small, charcoal-burning stove, making tea.

She would scold, "You shouldn't be making tea. You're a man."

Concern for her took precedence over maintaining male privilege. "I'll cook rice, Mother, so you rest a little more."

When he came home drenched in sweat from participating in sports, he would launder his clothes himself to avoid burdening her. Even when he came home on furlough from the Navy he continued to launder his own clothes.

"Aren't you ashamed of doing such things? A man shouldn't be doing things like that. Leave it there. Mother will wash for you."

"No, Mother. I love to do the washing. When we get used to it, it's really fun. See there! Isn't that clean now!"

In the summer of his second year of middle school, her health failing, she had gone by train to Takamatsu for treatment. He had accompanied her.

When the sun would shine in the window at which she sat watching the ranges of Shikoku, he would try to shade the window for her. When he heard the clerks approach with snacks he would run to them and buy milk for her. When she was tired, he would take off his wooden clogs and put them under the seat to incline it into a bedlike form.

At home on another occasion, he suggested, "Mother, let's go for a walk. After supper, let's go to the salt fields."

They had walked along the beach. Hashihama was wrapped in autumn mist. The setting sun dyed the peak of Mount Chikami a bright red.

"Mother, that's a cute little flower. I'll go and get it."

So saying, he ran and plucked a pure white wild flower and brought it roots and all.

"Truly," she said, "it is a pretty flower. Take it home and plant it in the field."

So on and on memories of him poured in on her.

A week after notification of his death, about the time he died at the stonewall on Niihau, she had a vision of his smiling face.

94

Allan Beekman at cenotaph of Shigenori Nishikaichi in Hashihama, Imabari, Ehime, Japan.

95

Puzzled, she asked her family, "Can it be that because Hawaii is so far away that it took this long for his spirit to return home?"

Six months after the death of Nishikaichi, a school teacher, Kazutada Hara, wrote a memoir of him that appeared in the form of a printed pamphlet. The spirit of the slain pilot reposed in the upstairs room where he had studied late at night for his entrance to the Naval Training School, at the altar beside which his photo stood. Offshoots of the wildflower he had plucked and planted bloomed in the yard.

A year following the attack on Oahu, the townspeople erected a cenotaph to him, bearing the inscription, "Here Rests His Faithful Spirit."

The cenotaph is a granite shaft atop four great granite blocks and towers 12 feet. A member of the *Hiryū* crew wrote the eulogy. Tribute is inscribed on front and sides of the shaft, with mention of his gentleness, filial piety, studiousness, dedication and bravery.

The eulogy summarizes his military career:

"... as a member of a fighting squadron, he participated in the attack on Pearl Harbor. It is honorable for flower and warrior to fall. He bravely attacked again and again, without fear of the fierce ground fire, destroying the fleet, even frightening the enemy. Having expended every effort, he achieved the greatest honor of all by dying a soldier's death in battle, destroying both himself and his beloved plane. Only 22, and having achieved merit in battle, he became in death a foundation of Imperial Japan.

"The Hawaii attack brought tremendous gain. Learning of it, the Emperor bestowed kind words on the fighting men: 'The utmost honor! Alas for the unreturned 29 planes! ...'

'... and awarded him the Blue Pawlonia Leaf Design Gold Medal Fifth Class. His meritorious deed will live forever.' "

Yet already the Japanese Navy, which had been sweeping everything before it, had met the check that, to the informed, meant they could not win the war. After they had secured the Dutch East Indies in early 1942, the Japanese planned landings at Port Moresby, New Guinea; Tulagi and the

Solomon Islands. They planned to establish a seaplane base in the Louisiade Islands, southeast of New Guinea. These steps were to lay the foundation for an invasion of Australia. But May 4-8, 1942, in the Battle of the Coral Sea, the American fleet counterattacked.

The Americans sank the light carrier *Shoho* and severely damaged the new fleet carrier *Shokaku* and inflicted heavy losses on the air group of the carrier *Zuikaku,* thus turning back the Japanese transports and so winning a strategic victory. The Japanese had sunk the carrier *Lexington* and damaged the carrier *Yorktown* and sunk a destroyer and oiler.

The Japanese had sunk more ships, the Americans had destroyed more aircraft. Nevertheless, the Japanese assessed the result as a tactical victory. Their confidence undimmed, they sought to lure the remainder of the American fleet into a decisive engagement at Midway.

But in the Battle of Midway, the outnumbered, outgunned American Fleet had turned the tables on Japan. The battle began June 4, 1942 and ended two days later with the Americans sinking all four of the attacking Japanese carriers, including the *Hiryū* and *Soryū* mentioned in connection with the attack of Nishikaichi on Kaneohe and Bellows.

The Americans killed 3,500 Japanese sailors and airmen, including the cream of its highly trained air force. It was the turning point of the Pacific War. Thereafter the Japanese were never able to take the offensive again. Bit by bit America drove them to the defensive.

In the Battle of Leyte Gulf, October 23-26, 1944, America obliterated the Japanese fleet. Japan was left with neither fleet nor air force with which to defend itself.

Then began the bombing of Japan, scientific and merciless. The area around the Nishikaichi home was devastated. The family realized the prophetic warning of Shigenori: never lose a war.

But as the tide of war turned unfavorably on the Nishikaichis, it left in its wake a situation in Hawaii more favorable to Irene.

9

THE SAD HOMECOMING

After the defeat of the Japanese at Midway, no informed person expected Japan to invade Hawaii. Influential residents believed that the need of martial law, if it had ever existed, had ceased with the vanished threat of invasion.

Particularly repugnant to some such liberals was the replacement of the civil courts by the military provost courts and suspension of the right of *habeas corpus.*

Only two months after martial law went into effect, a petition for a writ of *habeas corpus* was filed on behalf of Hans Zimmerman, on the ground that he was illegally intern-ed. The military circumvented an appeal to the U.S. Supreme Court by transferring Zimmerman to the Mainland and releasing him there. He could not return without military permission.

There followed a partial restoration of civil rights, which gave local attorneys firmer ground on which to base suits contesting the constitutionality of martial law. They filed a number of such suits in 1943.

Federal Judge Delbert E. Metzger issued a writ directing the then military governor, Lt. Gen. Robert C. Richardson, to produce two men in court who had been interned without charges. When the general, on orders from Washington, fail-ed to produce the internees, Metzger found him in contempt of court and levied a fine of $5,000.

Richardson responded even before the sentence was

rendered. He issued an order prohibiting the civil government from interfering with military personnel except to arrest those committing traffic violations. He prohibited all courts in the territory from even accepting applications for writs of *habeas corpus,* ordered cessation of proceedings in pending *habeas corpus* cases and imposed a $5,000 fine or five years imprisonment as penalty for any judge or official who might attempt to violate the order.

A compromise was finally reached: the general rescinded the order; the judge reduced the fine to $100. Pres. Franklin D. Roosevelt granted the general a full pardon and remitted the fine.

The two internees over whom this battle had been waged, described by the general as "dangerous to the public peace and safety of the United States," had meantime been sent to the Mainland and released.

In March 1944, a writ of *habeas corpus* was asked for Lloyd C. Duncan, convicted in provost court of assault and battery on two sentries. An even clearer test of martial law occurred in the petition for a writ of *habeas corpus* for Harry E. White, for in the White case there was no element of interference with the war effort. White, a stockbroker, had been sentenced by provost court for embezzling the funds of a client.

Presumably because they recognized the illegality of her detainment and anticipated that the power to continue her detainment would soon be wrested from them, the authorities permitted Irene to purchase her freedom. The price asked and paid was the signing of a statement absolving the government and all individuals concerned, from any liability as a result of her arrest and confinement.

After 33 months of internment, she returned to Kauai. She had only $50. The war was still in progress. Her relatives stood by her. Many whom she had considered friends shunned her, presumably because they feared association with her would undermine their security. Others, Filipinos and persons of Portuguese ancestry, regarded her with hatred.

When her brother-in-law, who had been discharged from the Army asked if he could do anything for her, she thought of going to Aylmer to see if something could be done about her liabilities on Niihau. She had received pay for her services, but only part of the goods she had left had been returned. Jewelry was missing. She had been expecting a big shipment on December 8. All these things had been lost.

Her brother-in-law drove her to the home of Aylmer in Makaweli. When she entered, Aylmer turned pale.

She told him of her plight and why she had come. She had given the Niihauans credit; she had left Niihau in such haste she had forgotten her Account Book. Would he help her collect what was due her?

He shook his head.

"Mr. Robinson, we're penniless, but I'm not asking for charity. I'm only asking you to help me get what belongs to me."

"I told you not to give them credit."

"But you hadn't paid your help in three months."

He remained unmoved.

While she had been interned, her children were being reared in the home of her sister, Haruyo, who had removed to Honolulu. Irene's plight seemed so desperate that at times she and her children thought of following Harada in death through suicide.

Only the Public Welfare wanted to help. In desperation she began to learn sewing. She established a shop and sewing school upstairs in a tenement building over the Tanaka Watch and Jewelry Store, operated by her relatives. She worked 15 hours a day. Bit by bit her situation eased.

Irene brought Taeko home from Honolulu. Later the other two children returned to Kauai. She kept a photograph of Harada by the Buddhist altar in the shop.

Aylmer wanted the bodies of Harada and Nishikaichi removed from Niihau. In 1945, she felt she had become able to give Harada a decent funeral. Japan had surrendered on August 14 of that year; feelings against her were less high than they had been.

She set about getting permission to bring his body, and that of Nishikaichi, to Kauai.

Permission gained, a group that included relatives of

Harada, a representative of the Army and a mortician from Koloa Mortuary set out for Niihau.

Much had happened to the Niihauans since Irene had left, at least some of it directly deriving from the incident that had cost her husband his life.

The day after she left, the Niihauans had wrapped the putrefying bodies of Harada and Nishikaichi in horse blankets to stifle the stench. They had dug graves about two feet apart and placed the bodies in them. The foreman bowed his head and asked forgiveness for the deceased.

They had filled the graves. At the head of each they had placed a rock about as big as a basketball.

The story of the bizarre happenings on Niihau had broken in the Kauai *Garden Island War Daily* shortly after Howard had given it to Aylmer, December 15, 1941. The Kauai Civilian Defense Staff issued a special order setting up a Naval Unit of the Kauai Civilian Defense Organization to be "composed of the courageous Hawaiians who defied an armed enemy on Niihau to bring reports to Kauai."

The newspaper spelled out the names of the crew that had rowed the lifeboat, erroneously naming Howard as its captain.

Lt. Col. Fitzgerald visited Ben at the hospital. There Ben and Ella told their story with Edwin Crowell interpreting and George F. Worts writing the account.

When the rescue squad had gone to the plane, some had wanted to cut out the Rising Sun symbol to take back to Kauai. Others began helping themselves to parts. Kobayashi had just taken a part marked "Made in U.S.A." when an American plane flew over and dropped a note.

The note directed them to leave the Zero intact.

On the evening of December 18, Thursday, an Army sergeant and lieutenant came to inspect the plane. They took photos of the Zero and took away some parts. They took the cannon shells of the plane down to the beach, placed them on the sand and exploded them.

About three weeks after the incident, Navy representatives came to inspect the plane.

Later still, the Army posted a contingent of soldiers to

Honolulu Advertiser photo of August 15, 1945

Ben Kanahele, left, shows the citation and decorations awarded him for his role in the Niihau Incident.

Niihau. Aylmer managed to have the commander strictly proscribe fraternization with the natives.

The national press had been quick to take up the story. Blake Clark included a chapter about it in his book *Remember Pearl Harbor*. He also wrote an account of it, "Never Shoot an Hawaiian More Than Twice," carried in the December 1942 issue of *Reader's Digest. Life Magazine* was so intrigued it sent William H. Chickering to do a story, but by the time he submitted it the war had moved on so the account went unpublished.

The incident inspired Hawaii's celebrated composer, Alexander Anderson to commemorate it with a song, "They Couldn't Take Niihau Nohow."

August 15, 1945, 56-year-old Ben stood in a drenching rainstorm at Army Headquarters, Fort Shafter, Oahu, where Lieutenant General Richardson read two citations by the late President Franklin D. Roosevelt for the part Ben had played in the defense of his country. Ben, "though unarmed, courageously attacked the armed and desperate Japanese enemy and, though three times wounded by pistol fire at close range, succeeded in disarming and killing his opponent."

When Richardson finished his brief message, the Rev. Henry Judd translated it into the aboriginal tongue. The ceremonies ended with Richardson pinning the Medal of Merit and the Purple Heart to the lapel of Ben's well-brushed blue suit. In his hands, Ben held a large certificate.

The band played, "They Couldn't Take Niihau Nohow."

The Army also accorded recognition to Howard. It awarded him $800 for the loss of his belongings in the fire set by the insurgents. He complained, however, that an outrigger canoe he lost in the fire was irreplaceable and should have been valued at $1000.

Howard enjoyed the celebrity brought him by the incident. A born storyteller, he liked to reminisce about the harrowing experience in which he had played so prominent and distinguished a part. Narratives challenge the skill of the author. A problem facing Howard was the difficulty of hav-

Maj. Gen. George F. Moore presents Howard Kaleohano with the Medal of Freedom. Fort Shafter, Hawaii, May 10, 1946.

ing Nishikaichi, the antagonist, express his thoughts freely to Howard, the protagonist, when neither spoke the other's language. Howard solved the problem by conferring on the pilot the gift of perfect fluency in English: Nishikaichi may have graduated from an American university.

An idiosyncrasy of the pilot made it impossible to introduce corroborating witnesses to this English fluency. When others were about, Nishikaichi fell into shy silence. Alone with Howard, the pilot felt at ease and became articulate.

In June of 1943, Howard returned, a hero, to his birthplace in Kona to visit his mother, Mrs. Abel Kaleohano, in Kaohe. He accepted an invitation to speak at the Hawaiian Civic Club of Hilo, which presented him with war bonds for himself and for Ben Kanahele.

This time, acccording to the account in *The Honolulu Advertiser* of June 7, he disclosed a new facet of the case. As Nishikaichi, in his plane, hovered over Puuwai, he started to machine-gun the people in the churchyard.

At Fort Shafter, May 10, 1946, Maj. Gen. George F. Moore would present Howard with the Medal of Freedom.

The war was over, the soldiers gone, though the Coast Guard maintained a radio station at the southern end of the island. Niihau had lapsed into its usual calm when the disinternment group arrived for the bodies of the insurgents. The Niihauans led them to the graves. The group disinterred the remains, put them in a small box and took them back to Kauai.

Irene had expected to bear the expense for the cremation of both bodies, and had expected the remains of both to be turned over to her. Accordingly she had prepared two urns. But the mortuary turned over to her only the ashes of Harada.

The family held memorial services for Harada December 22, 1945 and funeral services December 28.

Then Irene began to make inquiries for the ashes of Nishikaichi. Finally she insisted that she felt responsible.

Francis W. McKean, the mortician, told her, "The Army took the remains."

"Where did it take them?"

"That's a military secret."

The "military secret" yields to an examination of the records. In the records of Koloa Mortuary, Kauai, is an entry dated December 7, 1946, a year after the entry for Yoshio Harada, and concerns the cremation of one nameless "enemy war dead." The place of death is given as Niihau; the cause of death, "head bashed in." The order for cremation had been given by Lt. Pilke; the casket a "wood box."

It appears that the Army took the remains of Nishikaichi to the U.S. Army Cemetery No. 1, Makaweli and reinterred them there. On, or about, December 7, 1946 they again disinterred the remains and cremated them.

Army records show that the remains, identified as Unknown X-1, were shipped to Japan on SCAJAP Liberty Ship *James King V009* on December 12, 1946.

Since the remains were unidentified, the Japanese authorities turned them over to the Kanagawa Prefectural Department of Demobilization. The Office put the ashes with others grouped as "Unknown Soldiers" and stored them in a warehouse known as the Shrine of the War Dead.

The Niihau Incident continued to make occasional appearances in the English language press without, however, much speculation about the identity and antecedents of Unknown X-1.

In Japan there was skepticism about the official version of the death of Nishikaichi. An article entitled, "The Riddle of the Missing Plane" had appeared in a Japanese military publication.

June 29, 1953, Toyozane Maeda, Japanese vice-consul at Honolulu, sent an inquiry to the American Graves Registration Service. Though he incorrectly refers to the rank as lieutenant, instead of the actual posthumous rank of special duty ensign (*tokumushōi*), Maeda recognizes that Nishikaichi had been killed on Niihau. "... I would like to verify whether Unknown -1 ... and Lieutenant Nishikaichi are the same person."

The American Graves Registration answered, "... this headquarters cannot verify that Unknown X-1 who died on

Niihau Island and Lieutenant Nishikaichi are one and the same person.''

In 1953, someone brought a visitor from Japan to Irene, the first from Japan to call since before the war. The visitor was Mitsuo Fuchida, who had led the attack on Pearl Harbor and Oahu.

Since the day his subordinate had landed on Niihau, a great change had been wrought on Fuchida. He had had one miraculous escape from death after another. He had survived combat in China. He had attacked Pearl Harbor expecting to die along with half of his men but had returned unscathed. Six days before the Battle of Midway, he had been stricken with appendicitis. His second-in-command took charge of the battle and failed to return.

Fuchida was on the flight deck, waving pilots off, when an American bomb blew up the ship and threw him into the water. With both legs broken, he floated for two hours before being rescued. He was at Hiroshima for a military conference the day before the atom bomb was dropped on it. He was sent to investigate with 11 men. Within two years all of them, except him, died of radiation sickness.

With the rank of captain at the end of the war, Fuchida had gone back to farming. But he was often called to Tokyo by Gen. Douglas MacArthur, Supreme Commander for the Allied Powers.

One day as Fuchida stood on the platform of Shibuya Station, an American missionary handed him a pamphlet, ''I Was a Prisoner of Japan.''

The pamphlet was written by Former Army Sgt. Jack Deshazer, a member of Doolittle's raiders, who had bombed Japan April 18, 1942. Deshazer had been captured and spent 40 months in a Japanese prisoner-of-war camp. He said a brief reading of the Bible had changed his hatred of his captors into love and concern.

A Buddhist who revered the Emperor as God, and who was dreaming of revenge on his conquerors, Fuchida was inspired by the pamphlet to buy and read a Bible. In 1950 he converted to Christianity.

He said, ''I believe the Lord spared me so many times; so

my life is now his. I have dedicated the balance of my life to serving him."

At 50 he began speaking English, he would always speak it with a bad accent, and travelled about as evangelist. He was returning from a 35,000 mile Christian tour of mainland America when he met Irene.

This deep-chested, rugged man reminded her of her husband. She told him how she had cared for his subordinate. He told her of the nine lives he had had.

Fuchida knew the pilot to be Nishikaichi, Fuchida knew how she could get in touch with the Nishikaichi family; it is almost certain that he told her how.

September 10, 1955, Japanese Vice-Consul Takegorō Sato visited Irene. She gave him a full account of the Niihau Incident as it concerned her. In his report of several pages, the vice-consul wrote:

"(The pilot of the plane) was Shigenori Nishikaichi . . . Shigenori Nishikaichi is said to be from Shikoku, Ehime Prefecture; he has a father, Ryōtarō, in his hometown."

(Again, he told her) ". . . I think it is good to visit Japan now and meet with your husband's parents, also with your brother and also with the surviving relatives of Nishikaichi, the man with whom your husband died. If you wish to go, I will try to help you . . ."

It appears, however, that she needed divine revelation to coax her out of her lethargy. She was to receive this requisite impetus through Hannosuke Toyama, a former newspaperman, now a minister for *Seichō-no-Ie* (House of Growth). He had become interested in the Niihau Incident and had come to call.

Even though she had visited Ehime Prefecture on the Island of Shikoku, she was unaware that this prefecture is also known as Iyo.

But she remembered the pilgrims of Shikoku and she thought that after Taeko graduated from the University of Hawaii it might be possible to actively search for the Nishikaichi family and report on Shigenori. All her children would be self-supporting then. She would have fulfilled the last request of Harada to "take care of things when I'm gone." She would sell the shop and use the money to go on a pilgrimage to the 88 sacred temples in Shikoku and thus, somehow, find the parents of Nishikaichi.

She told Toyama of her dream of making the Shikoku pilgrimage. "I'm sure that even though it will take many years, I will be able to meet his parents and brothers. Until then, I will keep looking for them."

He said, "Shikoku is much bigger than the eight islands of Hawaii and has ten times the population. You don't know the geography and to go around as a pilgrim to find a person would be a tragedy. You don't have to become the heroine of a tragedy."

She already considered herself the heroine of a tragedy. She may have resented the prospect of his attempting to alter her role. Nevertheless, she continued to listen to him.

"In our *Seichō-no-Ie* there is such a thing as *shin-sōkan*—meditation and prayer. While thinking of the face of Nishikaichi, close your eyes, pray and meditate on him. You will surely come to remember what he wrote."

So there by the altar dedicated to her husband, while Toyama chanted, she did as bid. As the chanting continued, she went into a hypnotic trance that brushed away the cobwebs obscuring the memory she wanted to recall.

In the message Nishikaichi had left her, she understood the first three Chinese characters as his hometown, the first of which was written as *wave,* read *ha* in compounds. She recognized the second character as meaning *stop,* read *shi* in compounds. The third character eluded her.

The characters for Imabari, the city close by Hashihama had failed to register as had most of the rest of Nishikaichi's message.

After 20 minutes of prayer and meditation, she said, "I remember. On the paper he wrote there was the character for *wave.*"

"It takes more than one character to make a place name. Don't you remember the name of the prefecture?"

To assist her recollection, he gave the names of the four prefectures of Shikoku. She shook her head. He then began

109

to give the old provincial names of the prefectures: Sanuki, Awa, Tosa, Iyo.

She said, "Yes, it was Iyo."

"We know it is Iyo and you remembered the character for wave. Let's pray a little more."

For five minutes she prayed with eyes closed, then said, "Sensei, I remember. There was also the character for *shō*.

On the blackboard she used in instructing her students, he wrote what to him seemed the most likely character for *shō,* the one meaning *right (tadashii),* with a horizontal line at the top. Since *wave (nami)* is read in compounds as *ha* the two characters could be read *hashō* or *shōha,* depending on which character came first.

Puzzled, he asked in what order the characters had been written.

"I don't remember. Mr. Nishikaichi wrote it in haste and may have made a mistake. But I feel that *shō* was different from the way you wrote it; the top line was missing."

He erased the top line and lo, the character had become converted into the one meaning *stop,* read in compounds as *shi.*

"I've got it," Toyama exclaimed, "It's Hashihama of Iyo. He must have graduated from Imabari Middle School."

After this interview, Toyama ferreted out details of the disinternment, reinternment and cremation of Nishikaichi. He even obtained a duplicate of the tag of the box of ashes. The tag was inscribed: Unknown—Niihau Island, X-1. In Honolulu, he gained the co-operation of the Japanese Consulate for his plan to return the ashes of the slain pilot to the Nishikaichi family.

They located the ashes of Unknown X-1 at the Shrine of the War Dead in Yokohama. About this time an inquiry had come from Nishikaichi's older brother, Michio. So the remains were positively identified as those of the pilot.

A friend of Toyama got in touch with the Nishikaichi family, which now claimed the remains. The ashes arrived in Hashihama April 17, 1956; the family held memorial services five days later.

In the meantime, in 1947, the mother of the pilot had died, calling, "Shigenori! Shigenori!"

So now the family reported these matters to the deceased.

The return of the ashes more than 14 years after the death of the pilot was treated as important news in Japan. The Honolulu Japanese language press also carried the story. The English language press seems to have missed the item altogether.

The grateful Nishikaichi family sent letters of thanks to Toyama and Mrs. Harada.

Their interest piqued by such stories, representatives of the Japanese language media began to visit her. Knowing that anything appearing in Japanese would contribute to her image as heroine, and still inclined to believe that anything appearing in Japanese would be hidden from unfriendly Western eyes, she gave them grudging co-operation. She dribbled out bits of information—a penny to this one, a five-cent piece to that, like a miser cherishing the deference shown his hoard but loath to part with any of it. She grieved that the public treasury was being enriched, even a little, through the depletion of hers.

There is no evidence that any of her interviewers received from her anything of sufficient monetary value to compensate for the time and trouble they spent on her. But as the questions began again, as they had during her internment, even though this time the interrogators were sympathetic, there arose in her the suspicion that they were exploiting her for financial gain. This suspicion would surface whenever anyone drew near to express interest in the incident.

10

AFTERWORD

In an official report, January 26, 1942, Naval Lt. C.B. Baldwin wrote: "The fact that the two Niihau Japanese who had previously shown no anti-American tendencies went to the aid of the pilot when Japan domination of the island seemed possible, indicates likelihood that Japanese residents previously believed loyal to the United States may aid Japan if further Japanese attacks appear successful."

In a climate where the local "Japanese" were already accused of disloyalty and aiding the enemy before and during the initial attack, this criticism is mild.

On the day Mizuha and Kobayashi arrived in Kauai with their prisoners, Secretary of the Navy Frank Knox said in a special press conference in Washington:

"The most effective fifth-column work in this war was done in Hawaii, with the exception of Norway."

He had just returned from Hawaii where he had investigated the attack.

To his audience, the words "fifth column" and "Norway" rang a message loud and clear. The term "fifth column" originated as a term for sympathizers of the rebel Gen. Francisco Franco during the Spanish Civil War, in allusion to a statement made in 1936 that the insurgents had four columns marching on Madrid and a fifth column of sympathizers in the city ready to rise and betray it.

The German dictator, Adolf Hitler, had so infiltrated with fifth columnists those areas he planned to annex that some, such as Austria, fell to him without a struggle. Norwegian Vidkun Quisling laid the groundwork for collaboration with German occupation forces before the attack on Norway began.

112

By indicating that the Nikkei of Hawaii were fifth columnists, Knox tarred them with the same brush used against Quisling and his followers. Newspapers carried the story with such headlines as "Fifth Column Treachery Told," "Fifth Column Prepared Attack" and "Secretary of Navy Blames 5th Column for the Raid."

February 19, 1942, President Roosevelt signed Executive Order 9066 granting discretionary powers to Secretary of War Henry L. Stimson and all military commanders under him to prescribe military areas from which designated persons could be excluded. This order uprooted 110,000 Nikkei from the West Coast of America and confined them in internment camps.

February 23, 1942, in a memorandum to President Roosevelt, Knox wrote, "You will recall that on several occasions at Cabinet meetings I have urged the policy of removing 140,000 people of Japanese blood from Oahu to one of the other islands in the group.... I shall always feel dissatisfied with the situation until we get the Japanese out of Oahu and establish them on one of the other islands where they can be made to work for their living and produce much of their own food ..."

Some in Hawaii echoed these views in even more extreme form. John A. Balch, chairman of the board of Mutual Telephone, Honolulu, issued a pamphlet entitled, "Shall the Japanese be Allowed to Dominate Hawaii." The pamphlet included his letters to military authorities urging the removal of "at least 100,000 Japanese ... to inland farming states; this exodus to be of a permanent character ..."

But the Nikkei in Hawaii had become so integrated with commerce and industry that most responsible leaders felt that drastic mass action against the Nikkei would disrupt and impede the economy. Consequently such leaders worked against such disturbance and persuaded the military it was unneeded.

Investigation would prove that opponents of mass evacuation were on firm ground and that the accusations of Knox were without substance. Some German residents of Oahu engaged in espionage. A Japanese naval agent, Takeo

Yoshikawa, operated out of the Honolulu Japanese Consulate. But a little more than a year after the attack, Colonel Fielder declared:

"I have been in charge of military intelligence activities here (Hawaii) since June 1941 and am in a position to know what has happened. There have been no known acts of sabotage, espionage or fifth column activities committed by the Japanese in Hawaii, either on or subsequent to December 7, 1941."

Later Robert Shivers, FBI chief in Hawaii, reported, "There has been no proven case of espionage or sabotage by any resident of Japanese ancestry in Hawaii—either before, during or after the war."

Even in the case of the few hundred aliens arrested, many were interned on nothing better than the ignorance and prejudice of their examiners.

The Niihau case is unique. In contrast to word-of-mouth charges of other pro-Japanese activities connected with the attack, the Niihau Incident furnished something tangible around which outraged public opinion could rally. Through suppression and distortion of some of the facts, the reports increased the favorable appearance of the Niihauans and made that of the resident Nikkei even more unfavorable.

Considering the hysteria and mob chant of the times, Mizuha as leader of the rescue squad, with Kobayashi as participant, performed a master stroke in public relations on behalf of the Nikkei. That he confirmed the faith of Col. Fitzgerald is shown by Fitzgerald, December 23, 1941, appointing Mizuha and another Nikkei, Lt. Burt N. Nishimura as his deputies.

Mizuha and Kobayashi continued in the Army; in due course they were integrated with the 100th Infantry Battalion, made up chiefly of Nikkei.

The good showing of the 100th led to the formation of the 442nd Regimental Combat Team of Nikkei volunteers who had the highest IQ of any regiment in the Army and came to be referred to as "probably the most decorated unit in United States military history."

August 9, 1943, Gen. Mark Clark's U.S. Fifth Army, to

which these units were attached, landed at Salerno, Italy and began its drive northward against strong German resistance. At 5:00 a.m., September 29, Captain Mizuha was trying to locate the exact placement of the German machine gun nests, about 40 yards before him, whose heavy fire was holding up his entire battalion.

As Kobayashi said of him, "Mizuha was a good man; he was always volunteering for stuff."

This time a machine gun bullet creased Mizuha's back.

He miraculously survived the wound; but he was hospitalized for almost a year and disabled for further military service.

A civilian again, he earned a law degree from the University of Michigan in 1947. He was admitted to the bar, held political office and served as district magistrate.

In December 1958, Gov. William F. Quinn appointed Mizuha Attorney General. Hawaii was admitted to statehood in 1959, with Mizuha serving as the State's first Attorney General. In 1961 he was appointed Associate Justice of the State Supreme Court.

By this time, though they had learned nothing from their wartime humiliation and degradation, the Nikkei had achieved a dramatic improvement in status. The splendid record of the 100th and 442nd, the release of evidence that the Nikkei had been maligned, the realignment of world powers that converted Japan from hated enemy to respected ally had wrought a change in public opinion.

In 1946 Congress made Chinese and Filipinos eligible for citizenship. In 1952 the McCarran-Walter Immigration and Nationality Act removed racial barriers to immigration and eliminated the ban to naturalization of those of Asiatic birth then resident in the United States.

After his wartime internment, Shintani returned to his family on Niihau. Availing himself of the new opportunity, he became naturalized as an American citizen November 30, 1960.

In the meantime, a case bearing on the Niihau incident had received clarification. The Duncan and White cases, each of which challenged the constitutionality of martial law in Hawaii, finally reached the U.S. Supreme Court.

In a six-to-two decision rendered February 25, 1946, the court held that martial law as exercised in Hawaii far surpassed the authority granted in the Hawaiian Organic Act.

The decision threw doubt on all 37,000 civilian cases tried in provost courts during the war. How much greater the doubt of the legality of the detainment of those against whom no charges were brought!

One wonders what the fate of Irene might have been had the civil courts been operating. One wonders, too, about the role she played in the Niihau Incident.

I first learned about her through the Japanese language press. February 19, 1964, from my home in Honolulu, I wrote her a long letter, explaining my interest in the case. There was much I knew about it that she did not; I supplied her with some of this missing information.

At the time, I was the local representative of the *Pacific Citizen,* published in Los Angeles, the official publication of the Japanese American Citizens League. Since it was obvious that the *Pacific Citizen* wished to favorably present the Nikkei, this position may have helped to diminish her distrust.

From this first letter of mine, correspondence and even phone calls resulted. She gave me slight asistance with an article, "The Riddle of Niihau," published in *The East* magazine, Tokyo, in June 1971.

I met her for the first time November 10, 1971 when I visited her in her dressmaking shop on the 2nd-floor of an old, deteriorated frame building in Kapaa, Kauai. She looked younger than I had expected, in excellent health, with unusually good teeth for a woman of her age.

She accompanied me to the reception room. We sat down in wicker chairs. On the table were three photographs—of a young man, a young woman in nurse's cap, another girl.

"These are my children," she said. She spoke in a high-pitched voice, her words heavily accented. She gave their names.

"People come to me for information. They say, 'Don't

you want to make a lot of money?' I tell them, 'No. For the sake of my children, I don't want any publicity.' "

"And Mr. Robinson never gave me any help, though we lost everything on Niihau."

I was to learn that this difficulty with the Robinson family was one of the things about which she talked freely.

On the morning of the 13th, I called on her again. We talked for more than three hours. She became more and more at ease, using many gestures as she talked.

Her conversation tended to ramble, but these ramblings gave me insight into her nature. She always spoke of the pilot with respect. She complained that it was hard to control some of her pupils. They were untrained in *shūshin,* the system of moral ethics with which her generation had been indoctrinated, which taught such things as courtesy, filial piety, respect for age and for the law.

I had written a detective story based on the superstition of the dog spirit (*inu-gami*) found in some parts of Japan. The dog-spirit was supposed to be a hereditary quality in some families. When the dog-spirit owner hated someone, or coveted something belonging to someone, he might cause the spirit of a dog to enter into that person, making him sicken and die.

She said with a serious air, "We used to see that when a child quarreled with the children of a dog spirit owner that that child might have fever and headaches.

"Now people are not so poor as they used to be. Everything is more plentiful. So the dog-spirit owners are less apt to be envious. So from not using that power, it has become weakened."

I used some of the things she told me about the Niihau case in a long article, "From December 7 Raid to Niihau Island," which appeared in the 1971 Holiday Issue of *Pacific Citizen.* It was the most complete, accurate and authoritative account of the case to appear.

I visited her again September 12, 1972. This time we talked for five hours. From this interview came another article, "Aftermath of Niihau," published in the Holiday Issue of *Pacific Citizen* that year.

Nevertheless, as I continued to research the case, eventually becoming the authority on it, she cooled towards me. Evidently she resented my violation of the principle of keeping things in two separate linguistic compartments; of my writing in English of things I had learned in Japanese. Because of this heresy of mine, she came to fear me. Though I continued to write to her, she ceased replying.

I wrote to her in February 1982, telling her I would soon visit Kauai for the last time before concluding *The Niihau Incident* and submitting it for publication. I told her the book would be printed in both English and Japanese. I already had the information for a well-rounded book, but I might be able to do greater justice to her and Harada if we had another productive interview. Along with the letter, I submitted ten pages of questions and assumptions. Concerning some questions, I already possessed the Japanese language accounts in which she is quoted, but I preferred to get the information directly from her.

I followed up the letter with a phone call to her from Honolulu. I was unsurprised by her lack of enthusiasm for another meeting. Nevertheless, when I phoned her from my hotel in Wailua, Kauai, March 30, she consented to have me visit her.

The most obvious change in Kauai since the Oahu attack was in the proliferation of tourism. Well-dressed Japanese tourists, many of them honeymooners, swarmed the island.

Aylmer, aged 78, had died April 2, 1967, leaving his estate to his close relatives. Still a power on Kauai, the Robinson family guarded its fief of Niihau as jealously as Aylmer had done.

Irene's home was a prewar frame cottage in a well-kept yard on a quiet street in Kapaa. The front door was open and she came to it when I drew up in my rented car. The sight of me shook her.

She had observed her 77th birthday the preceding month. She limped badly and had lost some teeth. She was to tell me she suffered from high-blood pressure and had had a stroke two years earlier. Her hearing had become impaired; she talked in an unnaturally loud voice. Occasionally missing something I said, she would cup a hand behind her left ear and bark, "Huh?"

She complimented me on my appearance, adding, "You must be making a lot of money."

"I'm not making any money."

Perhaps the denial encouraged her to believe I had called to exploit her for monetary gain.

The case had become more and more celebrated in Japan. Japan's NHK had broadcast a dramatization of it with Irene in the role of narrator. At the time of my visit to her, a Japanese TV outfit was in Kauai to film the story.

I reminded her that I knew many things about the case of which she was, or had been, ignorant; I had shared this knowledge with her without stint. Some compensatory candor would be appropriate.

Many of Nishikaichi's comrades in arms knew nothing about an order for disabled planes to land on Niihau; they believed he had landed there in defiance of orders to self-destruct. Both of us knew he was following orders, but her refusal to mention the purpose of his landing was damaging his reputation.

She began to argue emotionally and irrationally. She drifted into a harangue about Buddhist Japanese language schools. I avoided interrupting. She became more calm, talked of her health, her children and grandchildren. Finally she began to talk of life on Niihau.

After a little more than two hours, it being near her dinner time, we parted—cordially. I expected to continue the discussion next morning.

In the morning, it was raining hard. I imagined the weather to be an ally. The rain would cause her to stay at home; she might welcome my company.

The sound of her voice over the phone dashed my hopes. Overnight she had turned sullen and spiteful. She had more important things to do than meeting me. She had more important things to do than talking to me on the phone. My phoning was an imposition on her time. After 10 minutes of fruitless reasoning with her, I surrendered.

"All right," I said sorrowfully.

One sympathizes with a woman in distress. One feels outrage at the degradation the Army visited on her at Waimea. From our sympathy and outrage springs a wish to extenuate, and even justify, her behavior.

The Japanese tend to regard her as the heroine in the tragedy of Niihau. Over the years I had sought diligently for evidence to support this opinion. In the end, I find my quest vain.

Within the limits of her understanding, she has been loyal to her husband. She has shown a touching concern for the education of her children. She has fought valiantly and successfully to lift herself from the destitution resulting from her long imprisonment. In a case shot through and through with evasion and falsehood, her testimony has been reliable on points she had observed at firsthand and on which she chose to give it.

Nevertheless, by any standard, American or Japanese, she is wanting in the role she played. If she were concerned for the reputation of the man for whom her husband gave his life, would she not have made clear why the pilot landed on Niihau? Would she not have spelled out the reasons for his actions after his landing? If she had identified him by name, would his remains have gone unclaimed in Japan for more than nine years? If she had wanted to get in touch with his family, would she not have done so when Fuchida, and later Sato, told her how?

She emerges from the Incident as one who, having bet on the wrong horse, spends the rest of his life sulking over his loss. She has been uncaring how her obduracy has damaged others. The role in which she has cast herself epitomizes not heroism but meanness.

For her ill-starred husband, one wonders what, in different circumstances, life might have held for him. Suppose Harada had been an educated, highly intelligent man. Suppose he had seen through the fraud official Hawaii had perpetrated on him. Suppose he had ripped open the veil of alien propaganda woven by press, public schools, courts, radio and other apparatus dedicated to the swindle. Suppose

120

he had said to himself, "I have been defrauded. I am not a Japanese. I am a Hawaiian; I am an American."

Suppose he had gone a step further and publicly announced his conviction—enduring ostracism, loss of employment, ridicule, fine and imprisonment.

Then he would not have become involved in the Niihau Incident. Aylmer permitted no malcontents on Niihau.

Photo by the Rev. Howard A. Smith. Unidentified officer before wing of the wrecked Nishikaichi plane, 1942.

INDEX

123